Origins of Our Faith

The Hebrew Roots of Christianity

Third Edition

Rick Richardson

Order this book online at www.trafford.com
or email orders@trafford.com

Most Trafford titles are also available at major online book retailers.

Printed in the United States of America.

ISBN: 978-1-4120-0824-2 (sc)
ISBN: 978-1-4122-1487-2 (e)

Trafford rev. 01/26/2011

www.trafford.com

North America & international
toll-free: 1 888 232 4444 (USA & Canada)
phone: 250 383 6864 • fax: 812 355 4082

Acknowledgements

Special thanks to Susan Richardson for her love and support in everything I do; to Shomeir ben Magen for his help and contributions to this book; to Sue Abramson for proofreading; to Rabbi Daniel Lapin for being my friend and mentor; and to Rabbi Avraham Feld and many in the Jerusalem Orthodox community for their patience, gentleness and kindness.

Cover photo by Gary Richardson

For more information visit:
http://www.originsofourfaith.com

Origins of Our Faith

The Hebrew Roots of Christianity

Chapter 1
The Phenomenon

Something is happening. It is happening within every denomination of Christianity. It is not the work of any organization or charismatic leader. On a very "grass roots" level people are meeting in home fellowships and church Bible studies to study the Hebraic origins of their faith. Many others are reading their Bibles on their own, believing that they are all alone in their discoveries.

Although this development in Christianity seems to be quite expansive, it is also a quiet movement, much of the time going undetected. Yet, within the Orthodox Jewish community, many have noticed the movement and call it simply "the phenomenon."

David Klinghoffer in the Toward Tradition pamphlet, "Enemies or Allies?" writes:

> *"As the Evangelical magazine Christianity Today has noted, "The real story in the last 20 years is the founding of scores of small, grassroots, pro-Israel organizations that rarely get into the headlines. They exist to educate and mobilize their local Evangelical community to support Israel."*
>
> *Many groups go beyond supporting Israel, and actively want to learn from Judaism the meaning of their own faith. Organizations have been multiplying that seek to inspire Christians to return to their Judaic roots; these groups include the Restoration Foundation in Atlanta, advocating "the restoration of all believers to their rightful heritage in the Judaism of the 1st-century church"; Hebrew Ministries in Houston, which proposes that Christians observe the Sabbath on Saturday as Jews do; and First Fruits of*

Zion Ministries in Jerusalem, but with an American following, which likewise advocates Saturday Sabbath-observance as well as observance of the laws of kosher food preparation.

Here in Western Washington State, Christians gather each year at Ocean Shores, a resort city on the Pacific Coast, to observe the festival of Sukkot, complete with dwelling in temporary booths or "sukkot" and waving palm branches and citrus fruits as per Jewish tradition. Jews who hear of such goings-on may at first suspect an attempt to lure religiously uneducated Jews to embrace a version of Christianity concealed behind Jewish decorations – a shamefully dishonest tactic pioneered by "Jews for Jesus." But the folks at Ocean Shores don't mean to convert any Jews; there are no Jews in Ocean Shores. (As Toward Tradition's Rabbi Daniel Lapin has quipped, "I'm less concerned about Christians who perform mitzvot [commandments] like wearing a prayer shawl and praying to God than I am about Jews who don't.")

We are aware of no comprehensive study of this phenomenon, but the anecdotal evidence is striking.

This change is not limited to one branch or denomination of Christianity. There are some Pentecostal groups that are beginning to use tallits and shofars in their service. Other groups have become more interested in the Biblical Holy Days, but no matter how it manifests it self, the phenomenon seems to be found throughout every form of Christianity. While visiting a Catholic convent, a few miles from Jerusalem, I was describing the phenomenon to Sister Katherine, (the head nun), believing she was unfamiliar with the "Hebrew Roots" movement. I was watching her nod her head as I was saying, "There is a growing number of Christians becoming interested in the Sabbath and Biblical Holy Days." She then said, "Oh yes, I attend a messianic congregation every Sabbath."

Messianic Jews?

In order to understand where this phenomenon is heading, we need to look into the origins of our faith. Christianity began as a messianic sect of Judaism. This is not to say that other religious Jews are not messianic, because clearly they are. One of the 13 articles of Jewish faith drafted by the thirteenth century Jewish philosopher, Maimonides, states:

> *"I believe with perfect faith in the coming of the Messiah; and, though he tarry, I will wait daily for his coming."*

However, there are a couple of factors that make Christianity different from other messianic sects of Judaism that have risen throughout the years. First of all, the size of Christianity is much more than that of other sects. Secondly, it grew and changed into something quite different from what it started out as, and did so very early in its development. It became a different religion. This causes us to ask the critical questions: Why and how did this happen?

As we will discover, Christianity began as "a bunch of Jewish guys", but because of the political and cultural struggles that existed at the time, difficulties arose as Jewish concepts were inserted into a Greek world without the experience or knowledge of how to properly assimilate them.

Why We Believe

In fact, our reality is often shaped by our inexperience or lack of knowledge about a particular subject. I had a teacher when I was in the 6th grade that told us a story about when he was a young boy, there was a map of North America in the classroom. The United States was green on the map. Canada was pink.

My teacher said he was shocked when his family visited Canada. The trees and the grass were green. Because of the colors on the map, he was expecting the grass and trees in Canada to be pink. The trees and grass in Canada were not pink, they never had been pink. And yet, up to his families visit that was my teacher's reality – that is what he thought was truth.

In addition, sometimes experiences and feelings change our reality. Have you ever known someone who had a strong belief in God, and then, for whatever reason changed that belief. There may have been a terrible accident that killed a friend or family member; something so traumatic that it caused that person to become bitter and lose their faith in an all powerful being. They may say, "If there is a God, how could he have allowed such a thing to happen?" Whether there is or is not a God has not changed. The man's BELIEF in God, however, is now the exact opposite of what it once was. This change did not come about because of intensive study and research. His beliefs before and after the accident are based on feelings and experience – not proof. This is not unusual. Most of our deep beliefs are not based on proofs, but on our feelings and our experiences, causing our "reality" to be less objective than what we realize.

A Matter of Perspective

Sometimes the real key to understanding requires no more than viewing our beliefs from a vantage point we may never have considered.

The reason for this is that our doctrinal outlook is derived through a particular perspective that is based upon certain assumptions. These assumptions are held as undeniable truths, locking us into a paradigm that is very difficult to alter. And, in fact, we will discover proofs that seem to support our paradigm, because we do not accept as valid any other perspective.

Let me give you a few examples of this. My wife and I were invited over to an author's home for dinner. He was a writer of "conspiracy books". It was an interesting evening of conversation, because he viewed everything in life as a conspiracy. That is the way he viewed the world. He also found "proofs" for all his theories because he accepted as a core belief that the conspiracies were true. In other words, he believed that the conspiracies were true to begin with, therefore, he believed everything that happened was a result of the conspiracy which in turn proved that it was true.

Our viewing reality different than what it really is happens all the time. We've all seen it. In fact, it has been the comedic device used in many TV sitcoms.

One situation comedy that used this device almost exclusively was a show called "Three's Company". Every episode was basically the same. Someone would either overhear someone else talking or find something, and they would believe that the situation was different than it really was. And because that is how they believed the situation to be, every time something was said or done they interpreted the situation in that way. The comedy arose through seeing two people interpret a situation totally different from each other based upon their preconceived view of reality.

Fill in the Blanks

However, even when we base beliefs on specific Biblical texts we don't all agree on what we are reading. Have you ever wondered why there are so many religions, and so many denominations WITHIN those religions? How could this be? If we are all reading the same text, the Bible, wouldn't we all believe the same thing? The problem is, we have a limited text. There is much that is NOT in the Bible, so we must "fill in the blanks".

Most "core beliefs" are based on what is NOT in the bible. Therefore, how we fill in the blanks determines some of our basic doctrines. Belief in a rapture, for example, is based upon very limited, non specific text. It is a relatively new belief that was not part of Christian theology before the 1800's. It gained popularity in Christianity in the 1950's, and more recently with the popular "Left Behind" series. It is strange to think that such an accepted doctrine within Christianity has so brief of a history, and that before the 1800's it was not part of Christian belief at all.

How do "new" beliefs get started? Through our reason and judgment we develop theories and doctrines. Then we find supporting texts that will "prove" our doctrines, and continue to build more theories based upon the ones that we have "proven".

The more that we build on our original premise, the more of an investment we have. Yet, all of our development is based on how we filled in the blanks to begin with. Or to put it another way, we base a lot of our beliefs on what we make up.

Seeing is Believing

A few years ago on Hoshanna Raba in Jerusalem, we attended a lecture given by Rabbi Gold. He talked about the phrase, "If I hadn't have seen it I wouldn't have believed it". And said the opposite is even more true, "If I hadn't have believed it, I wouldn't have seen it", meaning that our view of reality is based on our beliefs we have BEFORE discovering the facts. Regardless of how clear the facts are, we often refuse to see reality in any other way.

The condition then that we find ourselves in is known as "cognitive dissonance." Regardless of what may be true, we believe those things that are comfortable for us to accept, and do not believe those things that are uncomfortable. To look at the possibilities of a different perspective, however, is critical to understanding what happened as Christianity began.

This new religion believed in the God of Abraham, Isaac, and Jacob, and yet had adopted many pagan beliefs and customs. Its new writings used the Tanakh (Old Testament) as its authoritative text by which it "proved" its positions. Then its leaders said that the authoritative text was not authoritative after all and they, in fact, were "doing away" with many of the principles found in the Tanakh: a contradiction that many Christians have no problem accepting.

How did a group of just over one hundred followers grow into the most influential religion in all of history, and what is this phenomenon we see developing within the Christian faith today all about? Upon arriving home from my first visit to Israel in March of 2001, I posted the following on my website:

The Phenomenon

> *Something is happening. In every denomination within the Christian Church there is a drawing – a tug back to the origins of our faith. We who are being drawn are seeking something, but we are not always sure what that something is. We are part of a phenomenon, trying to the best of our abilities to follow that tug that we believe is God Himself drawing us back to our beginnings.*
>
> *From my perspective, it is not necessarily essential to know why the phenomenon is happening, only to see that it is. It is somewhat like the movie "Close Encounters of the Third Kind." Many people feel like the character played by Richard Dreyfus. They are pulled toward Jerusalem. They are compelled to reevaluate, and begin to observe in a more complete way, the Sabbath and the Biblical Holy Days. Prayer and gratitude and*

an eagerness to learn are becoming more prominent in their lives. They find a kinship with complete strangers who are also being pulled the same direction, to the same end.

There is no organization that will control or contain it. It is not our doing – it is God's. That, however, does not mean that there will not be organizational attempts to take control and even take credit for the movement now a-foot. This, in itself, is the biggest obstacle that we are facing: to allow God to do His work, and for those of us who are leaders to be gentle guides; to not evaluate our own significance as of any importance; to not read ourselves into prophecy; to not focus upon our own accomplishments, as if they were the important factor.

When you get right down to it, none of us have the market on being able to even fully comprehend what He is doing. Every time I believe I understand the breadth of what He is doing, I soon realize I was only seeing the edges of a small corner.

What then are we to do? Should we sit back and ignore it, avoiding taking any active role? No, but neither should we force it into our individual areas of comfort and familiarity. We should be aware of, and watchful for, those people eager for followings: for the person who believes that God has given His truth to them alone.

As phenomenees and observers of this phenomenon unfolding, let us not be focused in narrow areas and subjects that will divide us. Rather let us focus on what unites us: the topics, issues, and values that we can clearly see we are all moving toward; asking each other for patience and understanding; being able to teach and be taught; not forcing or convincing, but gently guiding, directing, and educating in the service of one another.

The Paradigm Shift

This book is an attempt to explain "the phenomenon" that is now happening in Christianity through undergoing a "paradigm shift". If you are willing to put aside your preconceived beliefs, you may find a reality that is much different than you have ever imagined! One that holds an exciting future, while discovering the origins of our faith. Those origins take us back to a young Orthodox Jewish rabbi who taught for just over three years and died at the age of thirty-three.

To find out more about this young rabbi, Rabbi Yeshua Ben-Yoseph, we must look at his life and teachings in context of the culture, time, and belief system in which they took place. This discovery begins by asking a common phrase heard in modern Christianity, "What would Jesus do?"

Chapter 2
What Would Jesus Do?

The Name "Jesus"

Since the discovery of the Dead Sea Scrolls, many people have come to view the New Testament writings in a different way. Some scholars, like the late Dr. Robert Lindsey, believe that (other than Paul's writings) most all of the books of the New Testament were originally written in Hebrew.

But wasn't Greek the language used by Jesus and his followers? Can we know for sure what language Jesus spoke? Let's look at Acts 26 when Paul was on the road to Damascus.

Acts 26:14

> [14] *And when we were all fallen to the earth, I heard a voice speaking to me, and saying in the Hebrew tongue, "Saul, Saul, why do you persecute me? It is hard for you to kick against the pricks."* [15] *And I said, "Who are you, lord?" And he said, "I am Jesus whom you persecute."*

Notice whose voice this was and what language it was being spoken in. Most of the evidence we have today indicates that Jesus was a Hebrew speaking, Torah observant Jew, who conducted his life in a very Jewish way. Over the years, both his words and deeds have been presented in a very Greek way. Even the name "Jesus" is part of an inaccurate presentation. The Hebrew name *Yeshua* (meaning salvation), transliterated into Greek is *Iesous*, transliterated then into English is *Jesus*.

HEBREW	**GREEK**	**ENGLISH**
Yeshua	*Iesous*	*Jesus*

During his lifetime he would have gone by the name *Yeshua.*

The Christian Perspective

One of the problems that we run into, when studying the customs of Yeshua (Jesus), is that we don't always end up with the picture we would expect to find. In the Forward to Dr. Brad Young's book Jesus, the Jewish Theologian, Marvin Wilson writes:

> *Among many Christians, Jesus as a historic figure remains largely removed from Judaism and the first-century Jewish culture.*
>
> *This point was ever so starkly brought to my attention several years ago through a piece of Sunday school literature, which came across my desk. It was written for grade school children and produced by a leading denominational publishing house. The part which caught my eye was a full-page drawing of Jesus. He was depicted as a boy and shown going up steps leading into a building. Underneath the drawing was this caption: "Jesus was a good Christian boy who went to church every Sunday."*

There is a major problem in trying to educate children about being a good Christian. The historical facts do not support our world-view of what Christianity is all about. Therefore, in order to continue supporting a perspective that has gone a little astray, it becomes necessary to alter history by changing a few items and just plain not telling the truth about others.

After all ... if you were to have printed the caption "Jesus was a good Jewish boy who went to Synagogue every Saturday," it certainly would not really fit in our 21st century view of Christianity.

What Would Jesus Do?

Have you seen the bracelets that say "WWJD?" It is an acronym for: "What Would Jesus Do?" Would it surprise you to know that Yeshua (Jesus), himself wore his own kind of "What Would Jesus Do" bracelet?

We find a reference to this in the book of Matthew:

Matthew 9:20

> [20] *And, behold, a woman, which was diseased with an issue of blood twelve years, came behind him, and touched the hem of his garment:*
> [21] *For she said within herself, If I may but touch his garment, I shall be whole.*

And then again, in **Matthew 14:35**

> [35] *And when the men of that place had knowledge of him, they sent out into all that country round about, and brought unto him all that were diseased;*
> [36] *And besought him that they might only touch the hem of his garment: and as many as touched were made perfectly whole.*

What was going on here? The Greek word used here as "hem" is *kraspedon,* which literally means fringe or tassel.

Strong's ..... **2899. kraspedon**, kras'-ped-on; of uncert. der.; a margin, i.e. (spec.) a fringe or tassel:-- border, hem.

In the Septuagint, *kraspedon* is the Greek used for the Hebrew word *tzit-tzit*. Why would Yeshua (Jesus) be wearing tassels or fringes on his clothes? And why was everyone reaching out to touch them to be healed? We find the answer to these questions written in the Prophets. First, let's look at a messianic prophecy.

Malachi 4:1

> [1] *For behold, the day comes, that shall burn as an oven; and all the proud, yes, and all that do wickedly, shall be stubble: and the day that comes shall burn them up, says the LORD of hosts, that it shall leave them neither root nor branch.*
> [2] *But unto you that fear my name shall the Sun of righteousness arise with healing in his wings; and you shall go forth, and grow up as calves of the stall.*

Malachi is one of the last prophetic books written before the time of Yeshua. One of the interesting things in this passage is the prophecy of the Messiah coming with "healing in his wings." What is that talking about? The Hebrew word used here for "wings" is: *kanaph*. The word literally means: "an edge or extremity of a bird or army, or a garment."

Strong's .... **3671. kanaph**, kaw-nawf'; from H3670; an edge or extremity; spec. (of a bird or army) a wing, (of a garment or bed-clothing) a flap

The people living in first century Israel, seem to have understood this prophecy to mean that the Messiah would have healing powers for those who touched the wings or fringes (or *tzit-tzit*) of his garment.

Another prophecy about the Messianic Age (or millennium) says:

Zechariah 8:23

> [23] *Thus says the LORD of hosts; In those days it shall come to pass, that ten men shall*

take hold out of all languages of the nations, even shall take hold of the skirt of him that is a Jew, saying, We will go with you: for we have heard that God is with you.

The word translated here as skirt is the same Hebrew word: *kanaph*. This is where the fringes or tzit-tzit were to be. So what were these fringes and why do I say they are like Yeshua's "What Would Jesus Do" bracelet? There are two places in the Torah that give the commandment for wearing "fringe:" in Numbers and in Deuteronomy.

Deuteronomy 22:12

> [12] *You shall make yourself fringes on the four quarters of your vesture, wherewith you cover yourself.*

We have a bit more information given in **Numbers 15:38**.

> [38] *Speak to the children of Israel, and bid them that they make them fringes in the borders of their garments throughout their generations, and that they put on the fringe of the borders a ribbon of blue:*
> [39] *And it shall be to you for a fringe, that you may look on it, and remember all the commandment of the LORD, and do them; and that you seek not after your own heart and your own eyes, after which you used to go a whoring:*
> [40] *That you may remember, and do all my commandments, and be holy to your God.*

You see the reason that God gives for wearing the fringe is to be a reminder to do what is right, like the WWJD bracelets worn by many young people today. God said it was to remind you to "do all His commandments," to be, if you will, Torah observant. Yeshua, therefore, looked like a Torah observant Jew of his day.

What Would Jesus Say?

So, we have an idea of what Yeshua looked like; but what did he sound like? As we have already discovered Yeshua spoke Hebrew.

Greetings

Although saying "Peace be unto you" sounds very spiritual, it is actually a common Hebrew greeting. The Hebrew words "Shalom Aleichem" mean "Peace be unto you."

Luke 24:36

> [36] *And as they spoke Yeshua himself stood in the mist of them, and said to them, "Peace be unto you."*

The proper response would be to say: "Aleichem Shalom" or "Unto you be Peace."

Liturgy

Did Yeshua use liturgy? Some will point to Matthew 6:7 to say that, since Yeshua talks against "vain repetition," he is speaking about the reciting of prayers and liturgy. But let us examine what is actually being said.

Matthew 6:7

> [7] *But when you pray, use not vain repetitions, as the heathen do: for they think that they shall be heard for their much speaking.*

The word used in the Greek for "vain repetition" means to repeat something over and over or to babble. This was NOT referring to blessings or prayers. Rather, it was referring to a mantra like the pagans (or heathens) would utter, or unintelligible speech. Notice that he did not say "Don't pray as your fellow Jews do." So did Yeshua recite liturgy and prayers? Yes, he did. Let's look at a couple of examples.

The Shema

The *Shema* is considered to be the "Jewish profession of faith." It is a prayer that consists of three passages in the Torah (Deut.6:4-9, Deut.11:13-21, and Num.15:37-41). This prayer is said two to four times a day. Some speculate that this was the prayer being recited by Daniel, for which he was thrown into the lion's den. It is so important that the Mishna allows it to be uttered in any language (not just Hebrew). (M Sot 7:1) It is also the prayer that many Jews have said as they faced death at the hands of persecutors including many who went into the gas chambers of Nazi Germany in WW2. Rabbi Akiva, the second-century sage tortured to death by the Romans for his support of the Bar-Kokhba rebellion, was the most famous martyr to die with the *Shema* on his lips.

The **Talmud** records:

> *"When Akiva was being tortured, the hour for saying the [morning] Shema arrived. He said it and smiled. The Roman officer called out, 'Old man, are you a sorcerer [because Akiva seemed oblivious to the torture] that you smile in the middle of your pains?' 'No,' replied Akiva, 'but all my life, when I said the words, "You shall love the Lord your God with all your heart, with all your soul, and with all your means," I was saddened, for I thought, when shall I be able to fulfill this command? I have loved God with all my heart, and with all my means [possessions], but to love him with all my soul [life itself] I did not know if I could carry it out. Now that I am giving my life, and the hour for reciting the Shema has come and my resolution remains firm, should I not smile?' As he spoke, his soul departed"*

These scriptures were an embedded part of Jewish life in the first century, as they still are today. They basically describe the Torah observant Jew and what is expected of him. To make reference to this group of scriptures, you need only say the first word, שמע (shema), and it is understood what you are referencing.

When Yeshua was asked what the greatest commandment was, however, he went much further than to give the first word. He left no doubt as to what he was saying.

Mark 12:28

> [28] *And one of the scribes came, and having heard them reasoning together, and perceiving that he had answered them well, asked him, Which is the first commandment of all?*
> [29] *And Yeshua answered him, The first of all the commandments is,*

שמע ישראל יהוה אלהינו יהוה אחד

(Shema Yisrael ADONAI elohenu ADONAI echad.)
Hear, O Israel; the LORD our God, the LORD is One:

> [30] *And you shall love the Lord your God with all your heart, with all your soul, and with all your mind, and with all your strength: this is the first commandment.*
> [31] *And the second is like this, You shall love your neighbor as yourself.*

Here Yeshua is quoting two passages from the Torah; **Deuteronomy 6:4** and **Leviticus 19:18**. By doing so he expresses the major profession of Jewish faith and emphasizes monotheism as the first priority of belief. He also supports the most basic passage in Jewish liturgy.

Blessings

In the Gospel accounts we also see Yeshua saying various blessings especially over bread and wine. Do we know what Yeshua would have said? Yes, we do. We have no reason to believe that Yeshua would have given a "new" or "different" blessing. Rather, his pattern was to follow the standard customs of the Jewish faith.

Luke 24:30

> [30] *And it came to pass, as he sat and ate with them, he took the bread and blessed, and broke and gave it to them.*

The blessing for the bread is:

Baruch ata Adonai Eloheynu Melech Ha olam
Ha Motzi Lechem min haAretz

Blessed are you, Adonai our God, king of the universe
Who brings forth bread from the earth.

The blessing for the wine is similar:

Baruch ata Adonai Eloheynu Melech Ha olam
Boree peri haga fen

Blessed are you, Adonai our God, king of the universe
Who creates the fruit of the vine.

So we have seen what Yeshua looked like and what he sounded like. But what were his actions? How did he live his life? Let's begin by looking at his birth and childhood.

... As Was His Custom

Luke 2:21

> [21] *And when eight days were accomplished for the circumcising of the child, his name was called Yeshua, which was so named of the angel before he was conceived in the womb.*

> **Genesis 17:10**
>
> > [10] *This is my covenant, which you shall keep, between me and you and your seed after you; Every man child among you shall be circumcised.*
> > [11] *And you shall circumcise the flesh of your foreskin; and it shall be a token of the covenant between me and you.*

We continue reading in **Luke 2:22**.

> [22] *And when the days of her purification according to the law of Moses were accomplished, they brought him to Jerusalem, to present him to the LORD;*
> [23] *(As it is written in the law of the LORD, Every male that opens the womb shall be called holy to the LORD;)*
> [24] *And to offer a sacrifice according to that which is said in the law of the LORD, a pair of turtledoves, or two young pigeons.*

We find this commandment in **Leviticus 12:6**.

> [6] *And when the days of her purifying are fulfilled, for a son, or for a daughter, she shall bring a lamb of the first year for a burnt offering, and a young pigeon, or a turtledove, for a sin offering, to the door of the tabernacle of the congregation, to the priest:*

[7] Who shall offer it before the LORD, and make an atonement for her; and she shall be cleansed from the issue of her blood. This is the law for her that has born a male or a female.
[8] And if she is not able to bring a lamb, then she shall bring two turtles, or two young pigeons; the one for the burnt offering, and the other for a sin offering: and the priest shall make an atonement for her, and she shall be clean.

From this passage most people believe that Yeshua's parents could not afford the larger offering and, instead, gave the less expensive offering we read about in Lev.12:8 (but again strictly following the Torah). Again, let's go to the book of Luke.

Luke 2:39

[39] And when they had performed all things according to the law of the LORD, they returned into Galilee, to their own city Nazareth.

We see that Yeshua's parents were very careful at the time of his birth to do "all things according to the (Torah) law." Let's continue on in the book of Luke and see a small bit of his childhood.

Luke 2:41

[41] Now his parents went to Jerusalem every year at the feast of the Passover.
[42] And when he was twelve years old, they went up to Jerusalem after the custom of the feast.

Leviticus 23:4

> [4] *These are the feasts of the LORD, even holy convocations, which you shall proclaim in their seasons.*
> [5] *In the fourteenth day of the first month at even is the Lord's Passover.*
> [6] *And on the fifteenth day of the same month is the feast of unleavened bread to the LORD: seven days you must eat unleavened bread.*

Deuteronomy 16:16

> [16] *Three times in a year shall all your males appear before the LORD your God in the place which he shall choose; in the feast of unleavened bread, and in the feast of weeks, and in the feast of tabernacles: and they shall not appear before the LORD empty.*

Again, here Yeshua's parents follow the teachings in the Torah, making a pilgrimage to keep the Feast of Matzah (Unleavened Bread) in Jerusalem. In addition to these holidays, Yeshua also observed a winter festival.

John 10:22

> [22] A*nd it was at Jerusalem the* ***feast of dedication****,*
> *and it was winter.*
> [23] *And Yeshua walked in the Temple in Solomon's porch.*

The Hebrew word for dedication is **Hannukah**.

Yeshuah did NOT observe Christmas, although it was observed (by a different name) by the pagans of his time. We'll talk more about that in a later chapter.

Let's take a look at one more scripture concerning Yeshua's customs before moving on.

Luke 4:16

> [16] *And he came to Nazareth, where he had been brought up: and, as his custom was, he went into the synagogue on the Sabbath day, and stood up to read.*

So we see that through his childhood and up until at least his ministry he was brought up to be Torah observant. But what was his attitude about the law of God?

Chapter 3
What is Law?

The Conflict

When reading about Yeshua's attitude toward the Law, there may be some surprises.

In fact, reading the Bible strictly as it is written may be somewhat problematic, because by doing so, we are confronted with beliefs and practices that seem to run contrary to many of the teachings of Christianity.

Many people believe that you should keep God's laws because you WANT to, not because you HAVE to. This is why there are those who believe that Jesus (Yeshua) "did away" with the law. Because if you HAVE to keep the law, THAT would be legalism, and being "legalistic" is one of the worst "sins" a person could commit.

This baffling view of law leaves Christians with the "freedom" to approach the laws of God like a buffet of arbitrary rules to pick through.

Although having a desire to be obedient is good, it does not negate obedience itself. Why do people look at the law this way? What IS the law, and how did Yeshua (Jesus) view the law? If we try to live our lives according to the law, is that being legalistic? What SHOULD our attitude about the law be?

Impossible to Keep?

There are those who say, "It's impossible to keep the law." That's why Jesus came; to keep the law so we wouldn't have to. Is that true? Is the law impossible to keep? Why would God create laws that couldn't be kept? What does God tell us about our ability to keep the law?

Deuteronomy 30:11-16

> [11] *For this commandment which I command you today is not too difficult for you, nor is it out of reach.*
> [12] *It is not in heaven, that you should say, "Who shall go up to heaven for us, and bring it to us, that we may hear it and do it?"*
> [13] *Neither is it beyond the sea, that you shall say, "Who shall go across the sea for us, that we may hear it and do it?"*
> [14] *But the word is very close to you, in your mouth and in your heart, that you may do it.*
> [15] *See, I have set before you today life and good, and death and evil.*
> [16] *In that I command you this day to love the LORD your God, to walk in his ways, and to keep his commandments and his statutes and his judgments, that you may live and multiply: and the LORD your God shall bless you in the land where you go to possess it.*

So, according to God, keeping his laws is well within our ability and, if we do so, our lives will go better. It should not be a "hard" thing to do. In fact, the law should be our most valued gift from God.

But didn't Jesus (Yeshua) teach that the law should be "done away"? Let's take a look at Yeshua's opinion of God's law.

The Devil Made Me Do It

In Luke 4:1, we see an interesting passage where HaSatan tempts Yeshua. Yeshua repels and gains victory over the adversary through his knowledge of the Torah, using it as an authority of truth. Let's look at this event and the words spoken by Yeshua and go back to the Torah and see what the context of these scriptures are.

Luke 4:1

[1]*And Yeshua being full of the Holy Spirit returned from Jordan, and was led by the Spirit into the wilderness,*
[2]*Being forty days tempted of the devil. And in those days he ate nothing: and when they had ended, afterward he was hungry.*
[3]*And the devil said to him, If you are the Son of God, command this stone that it be made bread.*
[4]*And Yeshua answered him, saying, It is written, That man shall not live by bread alone, but by every word of God.*

Deuteronomy 8:3

[3]*And he humbled you, and suffered you to hunger, and fed you with manna, which you knew not, neither did your fathers know; that he might make you know that man does not live by bread only, but by every word that proceeds out of the mouth of the LORD does man live.*

Continuing in **Luke 4:5**.

[5]*And the devil, taking him up to a high mountain, showed to him all the kingdoms of the world in a moment of time.*
[6]*And the devil said to him, "All this power will I give you, and the glory of them: for that is delivered to me; and to whomsoever I will I give it.*
[7]*If you therefore will worship me, all shall be yours."*
[8]*And Yeshua answered and said to him, Get behind me, Satan: for it is written, You shall*

worship the Lord your God, and him only shall you serve.

Deuteronomy 6:12

> [12]*Then beware unless you forget the LORD, which brought you forth out of the land of Egypt, from the house of bondage.*
> [13]*You shall fear the LORD your God, and serve him (only), and shall swear by his name.*

Continuing again in **Luke 4:9**.

> [9] *And he brought him to Jerusalem, and set him on a pinnacle of the temple, and said to him, If you are the Son of God, cast yourself down from here:*
> [10] *For it is written, He shall give his angels charge over you, to keep you:*
> [11] *And in their hands they shall bear you up, unless at any time you dash your foot against a stone.*
> [12] *And Yeshua answering said to him, It is said, You shall not tempt the Lord your God.*

And let's go back again to Deuteronomy.

Deuteronomy 6:16

> [16] *You shall not tempt the LORD your God, as you tempted him in Massah.*
> [17] *You shall diligently keep the commandments of the LORD your God, and his testimonies, and his statutes, which he has commanded you.*

And back to **Luke 4:13**.

> [13] *And when the devil had ended all the temptation, he departed from him for a season.*

[14]And Yeshua returned in the power of the Spirit into Galilee: and there went out a fame of him through all the region round about.

From the scriptures that Yeshua was quoting, how would you assess his view about Torah observance? Let's look at some of the basic teachings of Yeshua, and see what he had to say about Torah observance.

Keep the Commandments

Being an observant Jew of his day was not just something that he did in action and word, it also is what he taught others to do. At one time, when he was asked about how to obtain eternal life, his response was completely different than the one you would expect most Christians, today, to give.

Matthew 19:16

[16]Good Master, what good thing shall I do, that I may have eternal life?
[17]if you will enter into life, keep the commandments.

It is interesting to hear the response by this young man

[18]He said unto him, "Which?"

Now why would this young man ask Yeshua which commandments he meant? Wasn't he able to keep all ten? Well, that wasn't really the question being asked. He wasn't asking Yeshua which of the ten he should keep -- rather, which of the 613. According to tradition, there are 613 commandments in the Torah. Not all of the commandments, however, carry the same "value". When asked in Matthew 22 what the "greatest" commandment is he replies:

Matthew 22:35

[35]Then one of them, which was a lawyer, asked him a question, tempting him, and saying,

[36]*Master, which is the great commandment in the law?*
[37]*Yeshua said unto him, "You shall love the Lord your God with all thy heart, and with all your soul, and with all your mind."*
[38]*This is the first and great commandment.*

So the greatest commandment has to do with our relationship with God...

[39]*And the second is like unto it, You shall love your neighbor as yourself*
[40]*On these two commandments hang all the law and the prophets*

... and the "second" or lesser commandments have to do with our relationship with our fellow man.

Yeshua perceived that this man had a problem with generosity and his relationship with his fellow man, so he listed those commandments from the 10 that talked to that point.

Continuing in **Matthew 19:18**

[18]*... Yeshua said, "You shall do no murder; you shall not commit adultery; you shall not steal; you shall not bear false witness.*
[19]*Honor your father and your mother: and, you shall love your neighbor as yourself."*

Yeshua lists the last half of the Ten Commandments. The young man, assuming he was merely reciting the Ten, says:

[20] *...All these things have I kept from my youth up: what lack I yet?*

Yeshua then stresses where the young man lacked in his *HALACHA* or walk:

> [21]*...If you will be perfect, go and sell what you have, and give to the poor, and you shall have treasure in heaven: and come and follow me.*
> [22]*But when the young man heard that saying, he went away sorrowful: for he had great possessions.*

The Least of the Commandments

So we have seen that Yeshua stressed the importance of not only the Greater Commandments (love towards God), but also the Lesser Commandments (love towards our fellow man); but what about the Least of the Commandments (man's relationship with his environment)?

Matt 5:17

> [17]*Think not that I am come to destroy the law, or the prophets: I am not come to destroy, but to fulfill.**
> [18]*For verily I say to you, till heaven and earth pass, one jot or one tittle shall in no wise pass from the law, till all be fulfilled.**

> * There are two different Greek words here translated as fulfill. The first one is: pleroo, which means to make replete, or to make full. The second is: ginomai, which means to come to pass

> [19]*Whosoever therefore shall break one of these least commandments, and shall teach men so, he shall be called the least in the kingdom of heaven: but whosoever shall do and teach them, the same shall be called great in the kingdom of heaven.*

So Yeshua did not teach that one needed to just keep the greater and lesser commandments, but even the least. The commandment that is traditionally known as the "least of the commandments" is found in **Deuteronomy 22:6**.

> [6] *If you come across a bird's nest beside the road, either in a tree or on the ground, and the mother is sitting on the young, or on the eggs, do not take the mother with the young.*
>
> [7] *You may take the young, but be sure to let the mother go, so that it may go well with you, and you may have a long life.*

We see that Yeshua was NOT stressing merely the importance of the "moral" laws, but, rather, he was promoting the obedience of even the "least" of the laws (those whose purpose we may not even understand).

Now if Yeshua taught so favorably toward keeping the law (being Torah observant), why then do so many people believe that he did away with the law? Much of this misunderstanding comes from not fully understanding the culture and context in which Yeshua was operating; but much more has to do with just plain not reading the scriptures. In many instances, Yeshua was not teaching against the keeping of the law, but against the hypocrisy that existed in those who tried to USE the law TO AVOID KEEPING IT.

What is Law?

But what do we actually mean by the word "law"? When we talk about the law, we could be referring to a number of things. We could mean: a specific commandment, "the ten" commandments, all of the 613 commandments, the first five books of the Bible, known as the "Torah," or even extending beyond that to include the entire Tanakh (Old Testament). In general terms, however, the word "law" comes from the Hebrew word "torah" which means "instruction."

Much like a parent will give instructions to a child, God has given us His instructions. If we follow those instructions, our lives go better. If we do not follow them, our lives do not go as well. God has not just given us a few instructions on a small sheet of paper; rather, he has given us an entire instruction manual. If we really want to know how to live our lives in the best possible way, all we have to do is read the manual.

The problem is: we generally do not pay much attention to instructions or directions until something isn't working right. Then, and only then, do we take the time to read them; and, as soon as we are past whatever crisis we are in, we put the manual away until the next crisis.

What an amazing blessing we have. God's instructions for our lives are readily available for any of us to read and apply. You would think that we would all jump at the chance of knowing what these instructions are, and follow them as close as we could. Yet we, like children in adolescence, do not even seem to recognize the value and preciousness of the "instructions" we have been given.

Rabbi Pinchas Winston, in the book **Bible Basics** writes:

> *The commandments were given by God and are all in the Bible to teach mankind to achieve the ultimate satisfaction in life, through acquiring the character traits that are essential to living a fulfilling life.*

These instructions from God were part of His relationship with man from the beginning, and they were presented to Israel (as a nation) after they were redeemed from slavery in Egypt, as they stood at the base of Mount Sinai.

The Oral Law

According to Jewish tradition God not ONLY gave Moses the written Torah (Instructions) on Mount Sinai, but along with those written instructions God also gave Moses oral instructions.

In the first century a Gentile once asked Shammai, "How many Torahs do you have?" "Two" he answered. "One Oral and one Written, as it says:

> *"These are the statutes and judgments and laws [Hebrew: "Torot" i.e. the plural of Torah], which the LORD made between him and the children of Israel in Mount Sinai by the hand of Moses"* [**Leviticus 26:46**].

The Gentile said, "I believe you concerning the Written but not in regards to the Oral Law. Convert me on condition that you teach me only the Written Law." Shammai became indignant and sent him away. The Gentile then went to Hillel, who accepted him for conversion.

On the first day Hillel taught the alphabet: Aleph, beth, gimmel, dalet, etc. On the second day Hillel reversed the letters. The prospective convert disagreed and said: "Yesterday you taught me a DIFFERENT sequence." Hillel answered, "My son, you are relying on me anyway so rely on me concerning the Oral Torah too."

We would not know how to pronounce the Hebrew Alphabet if not for the Oral tradition. Similarly in order to understand certain laws we have to rely on oral tradition.

So in Judaism disregarding or rejecting the oral law is like getting an instruction manual, cutting it in half and throwing one half away. You simply wouldn't be able to understand how everything should work.

The written Torah (the first five books of the Bible) is part of the most well distributed text in history and available to everyone, but the oral Torah was transmitted from teacher to student generation after generation from the time of Moses. It wasn't until the danger of losing the oral law became a distinct possibility, that the oral instructions were written down.

In, the first century, however, there was no Mishna to open up. The oral instructions were known in the Jewish community, but unknown outside of it.

In **Romans 3:1** Paul asks the Question:

> *What advantage then has the Jew?*

He then answers:

> *Much in every way: chiefly, because that unto them were committed the oracles of God.*

Paul recognizes the importance of the Oral Law, which God gave exclusively to the Jewish people, giving them an advantage at living a meaningful and fulfilling life.

The early believers did NOT view the law as burdensome, rather, they viewed God's word and His laws as an authority of goodness and truth. It is through the keeping of God's laws that we find true freedom. I know that sounds like a contradiction, but it is true.

When God lead the children of Israel out "of bondage," what did He do? He gave them His laws. His laws (instructions) are our source of freedom. Imagine a society without laws. In a society in which everyone does whatever they want to do, will you have more freedom or less freedom? Well, obviously we would have less freedom. We would be constantly on the lookout for bands of street marauders that would rob and loot and cause destruction to property. And why wouldn't they? After all, there are no laws. It is only in a society that follows God's laws that a person is able to find true freedom.

John 8:32

> [32] *And you shall know the truth, and the truth shall set you free.*

John 17:17

> [17] *Sanctify them through your truth: your word is truth.*

As we have seen, Yeshua was a very Torah Observant Jew of his day, as were his disciples.

Frederick Holmgren, Research Professor of Old Testament at a Chicago Seminary, writes:

> *"Jesus embraced the Torah of Moses; he came not to end it but to fulfill it (Matt. 5:17) – to carry its teachings forward. Further, to those who came to him seeking eternal life, he held it up as the essential teaching to be observed (Luke 10:25-28). Despite Jesus' conflict with some interpreters of his day, both Jewish and Christian scholars see him as one who honored and followed the Law. When Jesus proclaims the coming rule of God, he speaks nowhere in detail about the inner character of this rule. He does not need to because that has already been described in the Old Testament and spoken of in Judaism."*

So why is there such a controversy over the observance of God's law? There are many truly sincere Christians who believe that Yeshua came to do precisely what he said he did NOT come to do: to abolish or "do away" with the law. (Matt. 5:17) Why?

Much of that answer lies in just seeing the attitude that we have about "the law." When we look at the law through a different set of "lenses," our understanding of the law can change dramatically.

Let's take a look at one of the heroes of the Bible who had one of the best attitudes about the law of God.

David

One of God's most beloved people that ever lived was King David. Why was King David such a phenomenal figure in the Bible? Was it because of his ability to keep the law? No, we can read of numerous times where David failed to keep God's law. God loved David, not because of his ability to KEEP the law, rather it was because he understood the awesome value of God's instructions for us.

Psalm 119:97 (מ)

> 97 *O how I love your law! it is my meditation all the day.*
> 98 *You, through your commandments, have made me wiser than my enemies: for they are ever with me.*
> 99 *I have more understanding than all my teachers: for your testimonies are my meditation.*
> 100 *I understand more than the ancients, because I keep your precepts.*
> 101 *I have refrained my feet from every evil way, that I might keep your word.*
> 102 *I have not departed from your judgments: for you have taught me.*
> 103 *How sweet are your words to my taste! yes, sweeter than honey to my mouth!*
> 104 *Through your precepts I get understanding: therefore I hate every false way.*

God's laws were in David's mind and in his heart. Despite the sins and short-comings that King David may have had during his lifetime, he is held up as one of the greatest figures in the Bible. He is one of the people whom God loved most. Why? Because he also loved God and his instructions.

Teach Your Children

We don't love our children only when we receive love first. We love our children no matter what condition they may be in. But when our children listen to our instructions, when they follow our words and carry out our wishes with respect and honor, as parents, we are very pleased.

Part of the Shema, we mentioned earlier, stresses the importance of teaching our children.

Deuteronomy 6:6

> [6] *These words, which I am commanding you today, shall be on your heart;*
> [7] *and you shall teach them diligently to your children and shall talk of them when you sit in your house, and when you walk by the way, when you lie down and when you rise up.*

One of the Rabbinical understandings of this verse is that the laws are universal instructions that were in existence while we were yet unborn (when you sit in your house); throughout our entire lives (when you walk by the way); upon our deaths (when you lie down); and at the resurrection (and when you rise up). In other words, the law of God is consistent and never ends.

So why is it that many Christians equate Torah Observance with legalism? Some will say that legalism is the strict obedience to laws and customs. Is that true? Is someone who strictly obeys the law, who is careful to follow the law in its fullness and to study its meaning and purpose being legalistic? No. Most of the examples of legalism in the Bible are describing someone who, through loopholes and parsing of words, nullifies the intent of the law.

When you, if you are a parent, tell your child, "You need to pick up your room," and you come back an hour later and the room is still a mess and the response is "Well, you didn't say I had to pick it up NOW," that is a legalistic approach.

When does the volume of laws in a society increase? When everyone obeys the law? No, the addition to law comes through disobedience; through finding loopholes in, and ways around, keeping the law.

Additional problems, however, are created by adding more laws resulting in the creation of more places to find loopholes and ways around the intent of the law. Good examples of legalism are found in our modern legal system. Politicians are also a good source of examples of legalism.

In his speech to the country during the Monica Lewinsky scandal, President Clinton made some comments that are worth talking about. He said:

> *"While my answers were legally accurate, I did not volunteer information. I know that my public comments and my silence about this matter gave a false impression. I misled people."*

In essence he was saying that he was following the letter of the law.

You Can't Legislate Morality

One thing to always remember is that even though something may be legal, it is not necessarily right. Paul makes this point in the book of 1 Corinthians where he says:

1 Corinthians 6:12

> [16]*All things may be legal to me, but not all things are acceptable.*

There is a phrase that is often misused that says: ***You can't legislate morality***. Many people will try to use this phrase to mean that we can't focus on morality when it comes to the law. Nothing can be further from the truth. That is what law is all about.

Laws define our morality as a society. The true meaning of the phrase, "You can't legislate morality," is: Even though you make something legal you are not necessarily making it right or moral. A good example of this is abortion. ***The morality of abortion does not change whether or not it is legal***.

Understanding the morality of the law is to understand the law's spirit. The spirit of the law is not negated through loopholes and technicalities. The letter of the law, however, can, at times, focus so narrowly on these factors that the law's intentions are lost.

Spirit of the Law

Let's explore the difference between the letter of the law and the spirit of the law. In Jewish terms, following the letter of the law would be keeping the law WITHOUT mitzvah.

In Putting God on the Guest List, a book concerning the Bar Mitzvah, **Rabbi Jeffrey K. Salkin** writes:

> *Mitzvot teach us to sanctify life. They foster altruism and self-esteem, so critical to the life of a young Jew. They can bring Jewish families closer to the Jewish people, to all people, and to God. ...So powerful is gemilut chasadim that performing acts of loving-kindness is the closest that humans can come to a genuine imitation of God.* [pp. 65,67]

Yeshua points out the "letter of the law" attitude that many had during his day.

Matthew 23:23:

> [23] *"Woe to you, teachers of the law and Pharisees, you hypocrites! You give a tenth of your spices --mint, dill and cummin. But you have neglected the more important matters of the law--justice, mercy and faithfulness. You should have practiced the latter, without neglecting the former.*

Do you see what he is saying and doing? He is showing the two aspects of the law: the part that is written (the rule or the ordinance itself), and the mitzvah (the justice, mercy and faith). *"You should have practiced the latter, without neglecting the former."* Far from saying that we should not be obedient to the law, he is saying just the opposite. We SHOULD practice the law, but we should also UNDERSTAND that the purpose of the law is to have justice, mercy, and faith among us.

An article written by the Jewish Organization, *Chabad House,* says:

"Cleave to Him"

> *We are told in the Torah Portion Re'eh, "Follow G-d your L-rd, fear Him, observe His commandments, hearken to His voice, serve Him and cleave to Him."*
>
> *On the words "cleave to Him," Rashi explains: "Cleave to His ways, perform acts of loving kindness, bury the dead, visit the sick, just as G-d has done."*
>
> *Rashi's comment must be understood: Since, according to Rashi, the verse means to tell us that we should cleave to G-d's ways and act as He does, why doesn't the verse explicitly state "cleave to His ways" rather than "cleave to Him?"*
>
> *Moreover, since the command to cleave to G-d's ways is stated as "cleave to Him," it is understandable that*

the ultimate unity with G-d is accomplished specifically through following G-d's example and performing acts of loving kindness.

In other words, the highest form of cleaving to G-d can only be accomplished through these latter actions, and not by performing the actions and commandments referred to earlier when the verse declared, "obey His commandments."

This, too, must be understood: All mitzvos bring about an attachment between man and G-d; what greater attachment is achieved by doing those things that fall under the heading of "cleaving to G-d"?

G-d commanded us to perform Mitzvos, and we perform them because we are so obligated. It therefore follows that the attachment achieved by performing mitzvos is one in which the performer is continuously aware of his own self; it is he who is becoming attached to G-d through his performance.

This is not so with regard to "cleaving to G-d." Although "cleaving to G-d" begins as the result of a command, the performance, completion, and totality of the command involves the total loss of any sense of self, for the person is wholly engulfed within Him – he cleaves to Him.

The difference between mitzvos in general and performing those actions that result in "cleaving to Him" is thus the difference between "attachment to G-d" and "cleaving to G-d":

This is a good explanation of keeping not just the letter of the law (or being legalistic), but also keeping the spirit of the law, where it becomes part of your very being.

The New Covenant

This is what we are talking about when we talk of "the New Covenant" mentioned in Hebrews 8 (quoted from Jeremiah 31)

Jeremiah 31:33

> [33] *"This is the covenant I will make with the house of Israel after that time," declares the LORD. "I will put my law in their minds and write it on their hearts. I will be their God, and they will be my people."*

How are God's laws written on somebody's heart? In the book of Matthew in the "sermon on the mount," we see an example of how Yeshua doesn't "do away" with the law, rather he makes the law EVEN STRONGER, condemning also the attitudes that lead to the breaking of those laws.

Matthew 5:21

> [21] *You have heard that it was said by them of old time, you shall not kill; and whosoever shall kill shall be in danger of the judgment:*
> [22] *But I say unto you, that whosoever is angry with his brother without a cause shall be in danger of the judgment: and whosoever shall say to his brother, "Raca," shall be in danger of the council: but whosoever shall say, "You fool," shall be in danger of hell fire.*
> [23] *Therefore if you bring your gift to the altar, and there remember that your brother has ought against you;*
> [24] *Leave there your gift before the altar, and go your way; first be reconciled to your brother, and then come and offer your gift.*
> [25] *Agree with your adversary quickly, whiles you are in the way with him; lest at any time*

> *the adversary deliver you to the judge, and the judge deliver you to the officer, and you be cast into prison.*
> [26]*Verily I say unto you, you shall by no means come out thence, till you have paid the uttermost farthing.*
> [27]*You have heard that it was said by them of old time, you shall not commit adultery:*
> [28]*But I say unto you, that whosoever looks on a woman to lust after her has committed adultery with her already in his heart.*

Yeshua at no point instructs his disciples to disregard or stop keeping the law; rather he uses the law as his *authority* and supports not only keeping the *letter* of the law, but the *spirit* of the law as well. Yeshua always taught obedience to the scriptures. Another name for the scriptures is the "Word of God."

In **John 17:17**, Yeshua says:

> [17]*Sanctify them through Your word: Your word is truth.*

Sha'ul (Paul) also writes (concerning the scriptures):

2 Timothy 2:15

> [2]*Study to show yourself approved to God, a workman that needs not to be ashamed, rightly dividing the word of truth.*

Keep in mind: the New Testament had not been compiled and much of it had not even been written at this point. So what then was Sha'ul (Paul) telling Timothy to study? Paul is confirming a long held Jewish perspective. There was no greater pursuit than to study Torah (God's instructions). John also says that the Word of God (the commandments) is a source of truth.

1 John 2:4

> [4]*He that says I know him, and keeps not his commandments, is a liar, and the truth is not in him.*
> [5]*But whoso keeps his word, in him verily is the love of God perfected: hereby we know that we are in him.*
> [6]*He that says he abide in him ought himself also so walk, even as he walked.*
> [7]*Brethren, I write no new commandment to you, but an old commandment which you had from the beginning. The old commandment is the commandment which is the word which you have heard from the beginning.*
> [8]*Again, a new commandment I write unto you, which thing is true in him and in you: because the darkest is past, and the true light now shines.*

We see that God's laws are not an arbitrary harsh set of rules that only Jews have to follow. Rather they are the guiding instructions for all of us. If we follow them, our lives will go better. If we ignore them, our lives do not go as well. The more we are willing to follow God's instructions, the better our lives will be.

Keep in mind, however, that we are talking about long-term benefit over short-term gratification. Most of the laws of God will not seem to be as beneficial in the short term. Is it better to cheat on an exam and get an "A" or to not cheat and get a "B" or "C"? Is it better to steal from someone else so you can enjoy a certain item, or to not have the enjoyment of that possession? Whenever we choose to disregard one of God's laws, we are choosing short-term gratification: whether it is cheating, stealing, lying, sexual misconduct, disregarding dietary restrictions, or not observing the Sabbath. We are choosing short-term gratification over long-term benefit.

But weren't the laws of Moses for ancient Israel? Christians don't have to follow them do they?

In a way, that is true. God told the nation of Israel that they were to be obedient to His laws, and they were to *be a light* to the other nations around them; BUT they were not to force others to be observant. Many Christians and Jews today, however, mistakenly interpret this to mean that Gentiles SHOULDN'T follow God's laws. They feel that somehow it is WRONG for a Gentile to follow God's instructions. *Christians often look at the laws of God as something bad and burdensome*, while *Jews often look at God's laws as only their exclusive possession,* which no one else should have the right to observe. This is a gross misunderstanding of God's intentions.

God wants to have the entire world turning to Him, with His laws written on their hearts: first the Jew and then the Gentile.

But didn't God reject the Jewish people? Isn't that why Jesus came – to start a new religion? Doesn't the New Testament condemn the Jews? Part of the biggest misunderstanding we have in reading the New Testament comes when we try to define the word "Jew." What and who were the Jews of the New Testament?

Chapter 4
Who is a Jew?

The Bible talks about a people known as "the chosen people". Who are they? Does God choose one group of people for a certain amount of time and when they don't work out, switch to another group? If not what is he doing? Is Christianity part of God's plan? If so, how does it fit into end time prophecy found written in the prophets? In a future chapter we will discus how these seemingly contradictory positions are all working together. In this chapter, however, we will focus on the question: "Who is a Jew"?

From: The American Heritage Dictionary of the English Language, under the word Jew it says:

1) *An adherent to Judaism.*
2) *A descendant of the Hebrew people.*

To be "a descendant of the Hebrew people" in simple terms would mean that your mother was "Jewish".

A Jew Without a Choice

If your mother is Jewish, you are a Jew. There is no way to reverse your Jewishness. You cannot "convert" to another faith and stop being Jewish. You would simply be a Jew with different beliefs. However, regardless of what your belief is, you are still bound by the laws that God gave your ancestors on Mount Sinai. You would still be expected to observe the Sabbath, eat kosher, and do many other things which are not required of someone who is not born to a Jewish mother.

A Jew By Choice

Beyond being born to a Jewish mother, there is another way to be Jewish. When a non-Jew accepts upon himself all the requirements of the law that are on the Jewish people, he can become a Jew. Today we call this process "conversion", yet it is much more than merely accepting certain beliefs.

This process has existed from the beginning of the Jewish people, when they left Egypt. Those who wanted to follow God were welcomed to do so. They were considered to be a part of Israel because of the belief system that they adopted, even though they were not originally part of the "family" of Israel.

Exodus 12:48

> [48] *"An alien living among you who wants to celebrate the Lord's Passover must have all the males in his household circumcised; then he may take part like one born in the land. No uncircumcised male may eat of it.*
> [49] *The same law applies to the native-born and to the alien living among you."*

The "alien" who wants to become a part of the Jewish people may do so, and be "like one born in the land". This means much more than changing your beliefs. It is as if you were actually "born again" as a Jew, with a Jewish history and ancestry.

Once a non-Jew decides to become part of the Jewish people and goes through the process to do so, he can never go back to being a non-Jew. So, by design, the "conversion" process is not a quick and easy one. There must be certainty of the individuals commitment.

This is the only method to become part of God's people or "kingdom". Yeshua confirms this in **John 3:3**

> *Yeshua answered and said to him, Surely, I say to you, Except a man be born again he cannot see the kingdom of God.*

The examples of the mixed multitude that came out of Egypt with the Israelites, Rahab, and later Ruth and many others who were not born as Israelites and yet BECAME Israelites, shows us that from the very beginning belief is how someone who is not a "Jew" can become a "Jew."

Paul refers to this in **Romans 2:28.**

> 28 *For he is not a Jew, which is one outwardly ... but he is a Jew which is one inwardly.*

Paul is pointing out that being a "Jew" is not confined to ethnic identity, but is also tied to a belief system that is available for anyone to adopt no matter what your national or ethnic origins are.

Beyond the basic understanding of what in means to be part of the "Jewish people", there are other definitions, or actually sub-categories, of being a "Jew".

1) Tribal
2) National
3) Regional

Without understanding and putting into context these distinctions, it will be impossible to understand how the Jews could possibly be fighting a war against Israel (1Kings 15:17). We could not know to whom a particular prophecy is directed (the nation of Israel or the nation of Judah). And parts of the New Testament would make no sense at all (like why the disciples of Yeshua, who were all Jewish, were hiding because they feared the Jews).

To understand the meaning of of the word "Jew", we must understand the context in which it is said or written.

Bloodline or Tribal

In probably the truest sense of the word, a Jew is someone who is a descendant from Judah, one of the twelve sons of Jacob, and a grandson of Abraham. To explain the story of Judaism or Christianity you have to go back to Abraham. Abram (his name was changed to Abraham later) is identified as a Hebrew,* meaning he was a descendant of Eber (his great, great, great, great grandfather).

> *Although the term "the Hebrew people" has become synonymous at times with the term "Jew," it would not be accurate to say that the terms mean the same thing. All Jews are Hebrews, but not all Hebrews are Jews.

God told Abram to move to another place. From this time on Abraham lived in a tent, never again having a permanent home. Because of Abraham's obedience to God and His laws,* God blessed Abraham.

Genesis 26:5

> [5] *Because that Abraham obeyed my voice, and kept my charge, my commandments, my statutes and my laws.*

> *Many believe that all of the laws of God were first established at the time of Moses. This is not accurate. We know this because Abraham is blessed for keeping God's laws.
>
> Before Sinai, God established laws for all mankind to live by known as the "Noahide Code." I will discuss this further in the next chapter.

Because Abraham followed God, there were some important promises made. It is through those promises that God will carry out the redemption of mankind.

Genesis 12:2

> [2] *And I will make of you a great nation, and I will bless you, and make your name great; and you shall be a blessing.*
> [3] *And I will bless them that bless you, and curse him that curses you: and in you shall all families of the earth be blessed.*

Abraham had a son named Isaac and Isaac's son was named Jacob. Eventually God changed Jacob's name to Israel. Jacob (or Israel) had 12 sons who became the fathers of the 12 tribes of Israel. One of those sons was named Judah. All of those who are descendants of Judah are known as Jews, just as the descendants of Levi are known as Levites. The descendants of Judah have specific blessings, recorded in **Genesis 49:8-12**.

> [8] *"Judah, your brothers will praise you; your hand will be on the neck of your enemies; your father's sons will bow down to you.*
> [9] *You are a lion's cub, O Judah; you return from the prey, my son. Like a lion he crouches and lies down, like a lioness--who dares to rouse him?*
> [10] *The scepter will not depart from Judah, nor the ruler's staff from between his feet, until he comes to whom it belongs and the obedience of the nations is his.*
> [11] *He will tether his donkey to a vine, his colt to the choicest branch; he will wash his garments in wine, his robes in the blood of grapes.*
> [12] *His eyes will be darker than wine, his teeth whiter than milk.*

From this prophecy we see that the kings of Israel were to come from the descendants of Judah, and the Messiah would also come from this line.

National

All of the 12 tribes of Israel in time became slaves in Egypt.

Exodus 1:11

> [11] *Therefore they did set over them taskmasters to afflict them with their burdens.*

Then God used Moses to lead the children of Israel out of Egypt.

Exodus 3:7

> [7] *And the LORD said, I have surely seen the affliction of my people which are in Egypt, and have heard their cry by reason of their taskmasters; for I know their sorrows;*
> [8] *And I am come out of the hand of the Egyptians, and to bring them up out of that land to a good land, unto a land flowing with milk and honey.*

Upon leading them out of slavery in Egypt, God gave the Israelites the Torah, or His instructions on how they should live their lives. (*Exodus 20*)

In time they settled in the land that God had promised them, and they became a kingdom.

King Solomon was the last king to reign over the entire Israelite people. Because King Solomon did not follow God in his old age, and built holy places for the foreign gods of his many wives, God told Solomon that he would lose the kingdom.

1 Kings 11:11

> [11] *Wherefore the LORD said to Solomon, For as much as this is done of you, and you have not kept my covenant and my statutes, which I have commanded you, I will surely rend the kingdom from you, and will give it to your servant.*

Upon Solomon's death the kingdom split in two.

1 Kings 12:19

> [19] *So Israel rebelled against the house of David unto this day.*

The northern kingdom was called Israel (it comprised 10 of the tribes), and the southern kingdom was called Judah (it was comprised of Judah, Levi, and Benjamin). The Northern kingdom (from the start) was not faithful to God's instructions.

1 Kings 12:31

> [31]*And he made a house of high places, and made priests of the lowest of the people, which were not of the sons of Levi.*
> [32]*And Jeroboam ordained a feast in the eighth month, on the fifteenth day of the month, like the feast that is in Judah, and he offered upon the altar. So did he in Bethel, sacrificing unto the calves that he had made: and he placed in Bethel the priests of the high places which he had made.*

They soon began to adopt the customs of the nations around them; something God had specifically told them not to do.

Deuteronomy 12:28

> [29]*When the LORD your God shall cut off the nations from before you, whither you go to possess them, and you succeed them, and dwelt in their land;*
> [30]*Take heed to yourself that you be not snared by following them, after that they are destroyed from before you; and that you inquire not after*

their gods, saying, How did these nations serve their gods? even so will I do likewise.
[31]*You shall not do so to the LORD your God: for every abomination to the LORD, which he hates, have they done to their gods; for even their sons and their daughters they have burnt in the fire to their gods.*
[32]*What thing so ever I command you, observe to do it: you shall not add thereto, nor diminish from it.*

In time the conditions had become so bad that the prophet Elijah believed that he was the only one in all of Israel that was not worshiping other gods.

1 Kings 19:13

[14]*And he said, I have been very jealous for the LORD God of hosts: because the children of Israel have forsaken your covenant, thrown down your altars, and slain your prophets with the sword; and I, even I only, am left; and they seek my life, to take it away.*

Finally God made the decision to send the northern kingdom (Israel) into exile. Because their idolatry was so great, their punishment was to be dispersed throughout the entire earth and to lose their identity.

2 Kings 17:15

[15]*And they rejected his statutes, and his covenant that he made with their fathers, and his testimonies which he testified against them; and they followed vanity, and became vain, and went after the heathen that were round about them, concerning whom the LORD had charged them, that they should not do like them.*

> [16]*And they left all the commandments of the LORD their God, and made them molten images, even two calves, and made a grove, and worshiped all the host of heaven, and served Baal.*
> [17]*And they caused their sons and their daughters to pass through the fire, and used divination and enchantments, and sold themselves to do evil in the sight of the LORD, to provoke him to anger.*
> [18]*Therefore the LORD was very angry with Israel, and removed them out of his sight: there was none left but the tribe of Judah only.*

The northern kingdom, sometimes called "the House of Israel" or "the Lost Ten Tribes", disappeared. It is one of the great mysteries of history. To this day there is no definitive answer to the question of their location. It appears that they have assimilated into the societies around them; never to return.

A central event, however, in prophecy IS the redemption of the northern kingdom (at the end of the age) and its reunification with the southern kingdom..

In the meantime, Judah (the southern kingdom) would, also go into captivity.

2 Kings 24:10 & 14

> [10]*At that time the servants of Nebuchadnezzar king of Babylon came up against Jerusalem, and the city was besieged.*
>
> [14]*And he carried away all Jerusalem, and all the princes, and all the mighty men of valor, even ten thousand captives, and all the craftsmen and smiths: none remained, save the poorest sort of the people of the land.*

The nation of Judah, however, retained its identity and returned back to the land after being exiled for a period of time in Babylon.

Ezra 1:2-3

> [2]*Thus says Cyrus king of Persia, The LORD God of heaven has given me all the kingdoms of the earth; and he has charged me to build him a house at Jerusalem, which is in Judah.* [3]*Who is there among you of all his people? His God be with him, and let him go up to Jerusalem, which is in Judah, and build the house of the LORD God of Israel, (he is the God,) which is in Jerusalem.*

By the first century (at the time of Yeshua) the southern kingdom had populated both the territory of the nation of Judah, and part of the territory formerly belonging to Israel. Also they were dispersed to other regions that were outside of this area, known as the Diaspora.

Regional

One of the most misunderstood definitions of the word "Jew" is that of region. To understand this, look at a map of Israel. The region around and below Jerusalem was the general area of the southern kingdom, Judah. This was known (in the first century) as the region of Judea. People who lived in this region were called Judeans. Above the region of Judea was the region known as Samaria, and above the region of Samaria was the region of Galilee. The people in Samaria were known as Samaritans, and the people in Galilee were known as Galileans.

John 7:1

> [1]*After these things, Yeshua walked in Galilee: for he would not walk in Jewry, because the Jews sought to kill him.*

It is important to note the distinction mentioned here is NOT between Christian and Jew, but between Galilean and Judean. So, the "Jews" that are mentioned here are people from the region of Judea, and not those who simply had "Jewish beliefs."

> [2] *Now the Jews' feast of tabernacles was at hand.*

Again this is a regional distinction. The area of Samaria lies between Galilee and Judea. The Samaritans also kept the Feast of Tabernacles. However, having adopted the practices of the northern kingdom of Israel, their feast was often celebrated a month later, as it is to this day.

> [11]*Then the Jews sought him at the feast, and said, "Where is he'?*
> [12]*And there was much murmuring among the people concerning him: for some said, He is a good man: others said, No; but he deceives the people.*
> [13]*Howbeit no man spoke openly of him for fear of the Jews.*

Again, it is important to realize that these visitors to Jerusalem were religiously Jewish. They had traveled to Jerusalem in accordance to the command in Deuteronomy 16.

Deuteronomy 16:16

> [16]*Three times in a year shall all thy males appear before the LORD thy God in the place which he shall choose; in the feast of unleavened bread, and in the feast of weeks, and in the feast of tabernacles*

They were also nationally Jewish. They were descendants from those who returned from the exile in Babylon. In addition, many of them were from the tribe of Judah. The "fear," however, was of certain people who lived in the region of Judea.

Who lived in the region of Judea? Judea was where the spiritual center of Jewish people was located. The Temple in Jerusalem was the focal point of worship. The sect that had control of Temple worship was the Sadducees; a group who rejected the oral tradition, (including the belief in a coming messiah).

The area of Judea was, to be sure, a place of much friction and unease. Even among the leaders of the general masses (known as the Pharisees) there was much division, especially when it came to the association with gentiles. It had only been a short time before this point in history that the Jewish people were threatened with assimilation. One of the prominent Rabbis to stand up against both assimilation and the ruthlessness of King Herod was Rabbi Shammai. Around the year 8 CE Shammai passed 18 edicts specifically meant to force separation between Jews and Gentiles.

Many of Shammai's views, however, were rejected by the followers of Hillel, another prominent rabbi of the time who was much more inclined to both associate with gentiles and accept them as converts.

The diminishing influence of the School of Shammai and the disappearance of the Sadducees happened when the revolt of 66-70 CE failed, and a "heavenly voice" in 70 CE was heard in Yavneh instructing the Jews to follow the rulings of Hillel.

The "school of Hillel" became the accepted view of Judaism (very similar to the early followers of Yeshua), while the leaders of what would become the Christian church became heavily influenced by paganism and their perspective grew more anti-Semitic as time went on.

Vince Garcia, in his article "What you never knew about the Pharisees" writes:

> *The greatest tragedy has been in Christianity's failure to realize who the true enemies of the Gospel really were, and thus Jews throughout the ages have suffered persecution by "Christians" who did not realize the real enemy died out in the 1st century.*

As you can see, the tendency for us to generalize about people and circumstances has caused us to misunderstand much of the history and conditions that led to our modern perspective and belief system.

There is much more that we could discuss on the issue of "who is a Jew?", but for now, we must ask an equally important question, "Who is a Gentile?"

Chapter 5
Who is a Gentile?

When asking the question, "Who is a gentile?" there is both the easy answer and the more complex answer. The easy answer is "Anyone who is not a Jew." But to understand what is being said in the New Testament we have to understand the context and meaning of the words being used.

Pagans and Greeks

For instance: go to the book of 1 Corinthians in the King James Version of the Bible and see the inconsistency found in the verses below concerning Gentiles.

1Corinthians 10:20 KJV

> [20]*But I say, that the things which the Gentiles sacrifice, they sacrifice to devils, and not to God: and I would not that ye should have fellowship with devils.*

1Corinthians 12:2 KJV

> [2]*You know that you* **were** *Gentiles, carried away unto these dumb idols, even as you were led.*

1Corintians 12:13 KJV

> [13]*For by one Spirit are we all baptized into one body, whether we be Jews or Gentiles, whether we be bond or free; and have been all made to drink into one Spirit.*

1Corinthians 10:32 KJV

> [32] *Give none offence, neither to the Jews, nor to the Gentiles, nor to the church of God:*

In the above verses, first we read that Gentiles sacrifice to devils. Next we read that the people that Paul is addressing

WERE Gentiles, (meaning they are NO LONGER Gentiles). Next we read that both Jew and Gentile are baptized into ONE body and we should be careful not to offend Gentiles. What is this talking about?

Let's look at the same verses in the New International Version

1Corinthians 10:20 NIV

> [20]*No, but the sacrifices of pagans are offered to demons, not to God, and I do not want you to be participants with demons.*

1Corinthians 12:2 NIV

> [2]*You know that when you were pagans, somehow or other you were influenced and led astray to mute idols.*

1Corinthians 12:13 NIV

> [13]*For we were all baptized by one Spirit into one body--whether Jews or Greeks, slave or free--and we were all given the one Spirit to drink.*

1Corinthians 10:32 NIV

> [32]*Do not cause anyone to stumble, whether Jews, Greeks or the church of God--*

We see that the word "Gentile" in the four verses out of the **KJV** is actually two words translated in the **NIV** as "pagan" and "Greek." From Strong's concordance we read the following definitions.

Strong's... **1484. ethnos**, eth'-nos; prob. from G1486; a race (as of the same habit), i.e. a tribe; spec. a foreign (non-Jewish) one (usually by impl. **pagan**):--Gentile, **heathen**, nation, people.

Strong's... **1672. Hellen**, hel'-lane; from G1671; a Hellen (Grecian) or inhab. of Hellas; by extens. **a Greek-speaking person**, espec. **a non-Jew**:--Gentile, Greek.

So then, ethnos means a pagan and Hellen means a Greek. Being a Greek Gentile is O.K. but being a pagan Gentile would not be O.K. Right? No, that's not entirely true. In the tenth chapter of Acts we read about some Gentiles who Peter visits.

Acts 10:44

KJV [45]*And they of the circumcision which believed were astonished, as many as came with Peter, because that on the Gentiles* also was poured out the gift of the Holy Ghost.*

NIV [45]*The circumcised believers who had come with Peter were astonished that the gift of the Holy Spirit had been poured out even on the Gentiles.**

*Notice that the KJV and the NIV both translate this word as Gentiles. Why does the NIV not use it's standard translation and say either "pagans" or "Greeks"? Because this is the word "ethnos" that normally would be translated as "pagans" in the NIV.

Who were these "Gentiles" and why is the word ethnos used here and not Hellen?

God Fearers

Let's take at look at the context of this verse.

Acts 10:1

[1]*There was a certain man in Caesarea called Cornelius, a centurion of the band called the Italian band,*
[2]*a devout man, and one that feared God with*

all his house, which gave much alms to the people, and prayed to God always.
[3]*He saw in a vision evidently about the ninth hour of the day an angel of God coming in to him, and saying unto him, Cornelius.*
[4]*And when he looked on him, he was afraid, and said, "What is it, Lord?" And he said unto him, "Your prayers and your alms are come up for a memorial before God."*

In the 1st century, Gentiles were divided up into a number of groups. There were pagans or heathens, who did not know the God of Abraham, Isaac and Jacob, and there were proselytes who had converted to Judaism. But in addition to these two categories of Gentiles, there were also *God Fearers* who, although not totally converting to Judaism, believed in the God of Abraham, Isaac and Jacob. Today they are also known as *righteous Gentiles.*

As we saw in the previous chapter, the School of Shammai did not believe that an ethnos (a Gentile who was not a full convert to Judaism) had a place in the world to come. Cornelius, being a centurion, would not be allowed, (under military restrictions), to become circumcised. Therefore, he would still be considered a pagan or heathen by the School of Shammai.

Kill and Eat

Continuing in **Acts 10:9.**

[9]*About noon the following day as they were on their journey and approaching the city, Peter went up on the roof to pray.*
[10]*He became hungry and wanted something to eat, and while the meal was being prepared, he*

fell into a trance.
[11]*He saw heaven opened and something like a large sheet being let down to earth by its four corners.*
[12]*It contained all kinds of four-footed animals, as well as reptiles of the earth and birds of the air.*
[13]*Then a voice told him, "Get up, Peter. Kill and eat."*

Many people point to this passage to support the belief that God has "done away" with the laws of eating kosher, but as we shall see this event has nothing to do with changing the kosher laws. Rather, God teaches Peter an important lesson about his relationship with other people, and how the influences of the School of Shammai caused an isolationist approach to Judaism that God had never intended.

Notice Peter's response when he was told to eat of these unclean animals.

[14]*"Surely not, Lord!" Peter replied. "I have never eaten anything impure or unclean."*
[15]*The voice spoke to him a second time, "Do not call anything impure that God has made clean."*
[16]*This happened three times, and immediately the sheet was taken back to heaven.*
[17]*While Peter was wondering about the meaning of the vision, the men sent by Cornelius found out where Simon's house was and stopped at the gate.*

Notice, that after having this vision, Peter could not figure out it's meaning. It was obvious to him that God was NOT changing the kosher laws. If that was the case, what was God trying to tell him?

Continuing in **verse 21**:

> [21]*Peter went down and said to the men, "I'm the one you're looking for. Why have you come?"*
> [22]*The men replied, "We have come from Cornelius the centurion. He is a righteous and God-fearing man, who is respected by all the Jewish people. A holy angel told him to have you come to his house so that he could hear what you have to say."*
> [23]*Then Peter invited the men into the house to be his guests. The next day Peter started out with them, and some of the brothers from Joppa went along.*
> [24]*The following day he arrived in Caesarea. Cornelius was expecting them and had called together his relatives and close friends.*
> [25]*As Peter entered the house, Cornelius met him and fell at his feet in reverence.*
> [26]*But Peter made him get up. "Stand up," he said, "I am only a man myself."*
> [27]*Talking with him, Peter went inside and found a large gathering of people.*
> [28]*He said to them: "You are well aware that it is against our law for a Jew to associate with a GENTILE or visit him. But God has shown me that I should not call any man impure or unclean.*

Again, notice what Peter's interpretation of the vision was. He did not believe God was now telling him not to follow the kosher laws. Rather, he believed that God was against labeling PEOPLE as unclean.

But, what law is Peter talking about when he says it is "against the law for a Jew to associate with a Gentile or to visit him?"

This is NOT a law found in the Torah. At this time in Jewish history, however, there was an anti-Gentile movement among the followers of Shammai who instituted the 18 edicts or measures.

In his book "Jesus the Pharisee" Rabbi Harvey Falk writes:

> *The eighteen measures were a set of rulings advocated by Bet Shammai in order to foster greater separation between Jews and Gentiles, these rules being opposed by Bet Hillel. [pg 56]*

Among some of the rulings that existed at this time was a prohibition of entering a Gentile's house (primarily to prevent assimilation). Also, eating with a Gentile was prohibited.

The opposition of associating with Gentiles still continued to be part of the custom of believers of "the Way." Even years after Peter's vision the disciples of Yeshua were amazed when Gentiles began to be drawn toward a belief in the One God in record numbers.

Acts 11:18

> [18] *When they heard these things, they held their peace, and glorified God, saying, "Then has God also to the Gentiles granted repentance unto life."*

What does it mean when it says "repentance unto life"? This means eternal life or life after death. The question that they were struggling with was, "Can a Gentile have a place in the "world to come?" Again, we see the conflict of opinion within the two schools of Jewish thought. The School of Shammai did not accept the concept of the "righteous Gentile," whereas the School of Hillel did.

Who is a "righteous Gentile"? He is a Gentile who follows the *seven Noahide laws*. Although he is not a full convert to Judaism, he does adhere to certain principles.

Chaim Clorfene and **Yakov Rogalsky** in the book "The Path of the Righteous Gentile" write:

> *With respect to God's commandments, all humanity is divided into two general classifications: the Children of Israel and the Children of Noah. The Children of Israel are the Jews, the descendants of the Patriarch Jacob. They are commanded to fulfill the 613 Commandments of the Torah. The Children of Noah comprise the seventy original nations of the world and their branches.*
>
> *They are commanded concerning the Seven Universal Laws, also known as the Seven Laws of the Children of Noah or the Seven Noahide Laws. These Seven Universal Laws pertain to idolatry, blasphemy, murder, theft, sexual relations, eating the limb of a living animal, and establishing courts of law.*

Can such a Gentile decide to become a full convert to Judaism? Absolutely. But, according to the School of Hillel, they should never be forced to convert or to proceed beyond those areas they choose. Taking this into account let's look at the "Jerusalem conference" in Acts 15 and understand what this discussion was all about.

Acts 15:3

> [3]*And being brought on their way by the church, they passed through Phenice and Samaria, declaring the conversion of the Gentiles: and they caused great joy unto all the brethren.*

What were the gentiles being converted to? Remember at this time in history there was no such thing as a separate religion known as Christianity. These were Gentiles being converted to a belief in Judaism, although they were NOT full converts.

> [4]*And when they were come to Jerusalem, they were received of the church, and of the apostles and elders, and they declared all things that God had done with them.*
> [5]*But there rose up certain of the sect of the Pharisees which believed, saying, That it was needful to circumcise them, and to command them to keep the law of Moses.*

Notice that they were NOT circumcised NOR were they keeping the "laws of Moses."

> [6]*And the apostles and elders came together for to consider of this matter.*
> [7]*And when there had been much disputing, Peter rose up, and said to them, "Men and brethren, you know how that a good while ago God made choice among us, that the* Gentiles *by my mouth should hear the word of the gospel, and believe.*
> [8]*And God, which knows the hearts, bare them witness, giving them the Holy Ghost, even as he did to us;*
> [9]*And put no difference between us and them, purifying their hearts by faith.*
> [10]*Now therefore why tempt you God, to put a yoke upon the neck of the disciples, which neither our fathers nor we were able to bear?*

What is this yoke that is hard to bear and who is it on? Is this saying that God's instructions for living a good life should be thrown out because they are too hard to follow? No, that is not what is being said. The followers of Yeshua from the School of Shammai were promoting the practice of forcing Gentiles to comply with aspects of the law they were not required to observe. They were saying that a Gentile had to become a full convert to Judaism before they would associate or fellowship with them. They (those from the School of Shammai) were putting a yoke upon those disciples (from the School of Hillel).

[13]And after they had held their peace, James answered, saying, "Men and brethren, listen to me:
[14]Simeon has declared how God at the first did visit the Gentiles, to take out of them a people for his name.
[15]And to this agree the words of the prophets; as it is written,
[16]After this I will return, and will build again the tabernacle of David, which is fallen down; and I will build again the ruins thereof, and I will set it up:
[17]That the residue of men might seek after the Lord, and all the Gentiles, upon whom my name is called, says the Lord, who doeth all these things.
[18]Known unto God are all his works from the beginning of the world.
[19]Wherefore my sentence is, that we trouble not them, which from among the Gentiles are turned to God:
[20]But that we write unto them, that they abstain from pollutions of idols, and from fornication, and from things strangled, and from blood.

James explains that Gentiles do not need to become full converts to Judaism to be acceptable before God. Rather, as long as the Gentiles follows the seven Noahide laws they should be considered righteous, and if they desired to observe more, they were welcomed to learn every Sabbath in the synagogue with the Jewish congregants.

[21]For Moses of old time hath in every city them that preach him, being read in the synagogues every Sabbath day.

The school of Hillel (along with believers in "the Way") promoted the idea of the Jewish people being "a light" to the Gentiles, and did not isolate themselves from them. That had been God's intention from the beginning.

Exodus 12:43

> [43]*And the LORD said unto Moses and Aaron, This is the ordinance of the Passover: There shall no stranger eat thereof:*
> [44]*But every man's servant that is bought for money, when thou hast circumcised him, then shall he eat thereof.*
> [45]*A foreigner and an hired servant shall not eat thereof.*
> [46]*In one house shall it be eaten; thou shall not carry forth ought of the flesh abroad out of the house; neither shall ye break a bone thereof.*
> [47]*All the congregation of Israel shall keep it.*
> [48]*And when a stranger shall sojourn with thee, and will keep the Passover to the LORD, let all his males be circumcised, and then let him come near and keep it; and he shall be as one that is born in the land: for no uncircumcised person shall eat thereof.*
> [49]*One law shall be to him that is home-born, and unto the stranger that sojourns among you.*
> [50]*Thus did all the children of Israel; as the LORD commanded Moses and Aaron, so did they.*
> [51]*And it came to pass the selfsame day, that the LORD did bring the children of Israel out of the land of Egypt by their armies.*

The mixed multitude that came out of Egypt with the Children of Israel could not eat the Passover. However, if they CHOSE to become a full convert, they would be allowed to do so. In fact that would be a great decision, but it had to be THEIR choice.

Romans 3:25

> [25]*Circumcision has value if you observe the law, but if you break the law, you have become as though you had not been circumcised.*
> [26]*If those who are not circumcised keep the law's requirements, will they not be regarded as though they were circumcised?*
> [27]*The one who is* <u>*not*</u> *circumcised physically* <u>*and yet obeys the law*</u> *will condemn you who, even though you have the written code and circumcision, are a lawbreaker.*
> [28]*A man is not a Jew if he is only one outwardly, nor is circumcision merely outward and physical.*
> [29]*No, a man is a Jew if he is one inwardly; and circumcision is circumcision of the heart, by the Spirit, not by the written code. Such a man's praise is not from men, but from God.*
> [3:1]<u>*What advantage*</u>*, then, is there in being a Jew, or what value is there in circumcision?*
> [2]<u>*Much in every way!*</u> *First of all, they have been entrusted with the oral law.*

What is Paul trying to say here? Again, we need to take into context the issue that is being discussed. A Jew from the School of Shammai would not have fellowship with an uncircumcised Gentile. A Jew from the School of Hillel, however, accepted the Gentile who was attempting to obey God through observing the Noahide laws, and yet remained uncircumcised. They believed (as do Jews today) that the "righteous Gentile" <u>could be saved</u> (have a place in the world to come).

He was certainly <u>not</u> saying that circumcision was of no value, nor was he attempting to tell a Gentile that he should not seek conversion, if he chose to do so.

The Law and the Noahide

However, converting to Judaism would not make the Gentile a better person. The Gentile is considered "righteous" by observing the seven Noahide laws.

1) Prohibition against idol worship
2) Prohibition against blasphemy
3) Prohibition against murder
4) Prohibition against adultery
5) Prohibition against theft
6) Prohibition against eating flesh torn from a live animal or drinking it's blood
7) Establishing a legal system

So the application of law is not the same for everyone. In the Mosaic law there are laws that apply only to women, others to men. Some laws only apply to Levites, and others to priests. When you live in the land there are laws that apply, that do not apply when you are not in the land. There are also laws that apply only when the Temple is standing. Likewise there are laws that apply to Jews (the Children of Israel) that do not apply to Gentiles.

The laws you are required to observe do not make you a better person. A male Levite living in Israel is not inherently a better person than a female Danite living in the diaspora. However, each person would have a different set of laws to follow. It is the same for a Gentile who is only required to observe the seven Noahide laws.
Chaim Clorfene and **Yakov Rogalsky** in "The Path of the Righteous Gentile" write:

> *By observing the Seven Noahide Commandments, a Gentile fulfills the purpose of his creation and receives*

> *a share of the World to Come, the blessed spiritual world of the righteous.*
>
> *...The Children of Noah are co-religionists of the Children of Israel. Together, they are peaceful partners striving to perfect the world and thereby give God satisfaction. By viewing himself as a Noahite, the Gentile becomes like the Jew, in that he is a member of a people whose peoplehood (not just his religion) is synonymous with its relationship to God.*

Rabbi Yakov Fogelman, in his April Torah commentary of 2003 writes:

> *... Jesus and Paul were good guys, not out to take Jews away from their religion (see Matt.5, Luke 16), but to bring non-Jews to theirs – the Noahide Code; all should remain in their own faith, both Jews and Noahides; later errant Christians distorted their message, tried to convert Jews and deified Jesus, which would probably have horrified him.*

In **Rabbi Harvey Falk's** book <u>**Jesus the Pharisee**</u>, he quotes Rabbi Jacob Emden concerning the formation of Christianity as saying:

> *But for the Gentiles, he reserved the Seven Commandments which they have always been obligated to fulfill. It is for that reason that were forbidden pollutions of idols, fornication, blood, and things strangled (Acts 15) They also forbade them circumcision and the Sabbath. All of this was in accord with the law and custom of our Torah, as expounded by our Sages, the true transmitters from Moses at Sinai. It was they who sat upon his seat (as the Nazarene himself attested [Mt.23]). It was they (the Sages and Pharisees) who said it is forbidden to circumcise a Gentile who does accept upon himself the yoke of (all) the commandments. The Sages likewise*

said that the Gentile is enjoined not to (fully) to observe the Sabbath. The Apostles of the Nazarene therefore chose for those Gentiles who do not enter the Jewish faith that instead of circumcision they should practice immersion (for truly immersion is also a condition of full conversion), and a commemoration of the Sabbath was made for them on Sunday.

Paul believed that he was living in the "last days", and if Gentiles were to believe and work for the coming of the Jewish Messiah, they would help bring the world into a time of peace. This would be to the benefit of both Jew AND Gentile. Paul also tells the Gentiles that they would be used as an important part of God's redemption of Israel (the northern kingdom that had become lost).

Acts 13:47

NIV [47]*For this is what the Lord has commanded us: "'I have made you a light for the Gentiles, that you may bring salvation to the ends of the earth.'"*

[48]*When the Gentiles heard this, they were glad and honored the word of the Lord; and all who were appointed for eternal life believed.*

How did this group of Jewish followers, many of whom believed that you had to become a complete convert to Judaism BEFORE you could be saved, eventually become "the Church" believing you should ABANDON Judaism for salvation?

We find the answer to that question by studying the journey Christianity takes from the Synagogue to the Church.

Chapter 6
From Synagogue to Church

When did the "Church" begin?

Many Christians will say that the Church began on the day of Pentecost in 30CE (AD). That, however, is incorrect. The beliefs and values, the laws and form of worship, and all of the basic elements of Judaism, did not discontinue after the death of Yeshua.

Followers of "the way" still went to the temple daily to fulfill requirements of the law (including animal sacrifices). For the first 40 years after the crucifixion, the followers of Yeshua did not view themselves as being separated from other Jews. They met in the synagogues every Sabbath among the other Jews of their time.

They continued to keep all of the annual Holy Days, such as Pesach, Shavuot, Rosh Hashanah, Yom Kippur and Sukkot.

What happened? A number of factors contributed to the radical change of beliefs and practices of this Jewish sect. They included an increase of Gentile converts within the sect, Roman persecution, martyrdom of its Jewish leaders, and misunderstanding of the time that they were in.

The End is Near

The earliest followers of Yeshua as Messiah believed that they were living in the last days. That may be why more time was not given to thoroughly teaching new "converts." They just didn't believe that they had that much time. We read references throughout the New Testament that show us how the first century (and especially the first generation) Christian felt that Yeshua's return was imminent.

Paul says in **1Thessalonians 4:15**.

> [15]*For this we declare to you by the word of the Lord, that we who are alive, who are left until the coming of the Lord, will by no means precede those who have died.*
> [16]*For the Lord himself, with a cry of command, with the archangel's call and with the sound of God's trumpet, will descend from heaven, and the dead in Messiah will rise first.*
> [17]*Then we who are alive, who are left, will be caught up in the clouds together with them to meet the Lord in the air; and so we will be with the Lord forever.*

The book of Joel is quoted in Peter's sermon on Pentecost in **Acts 2:16.**

> [17]*'In the last days it will be, God declares, that I will pour out my Spirit upon all flesh, and your sons and your daughters shall prophesy, and your young men shall see visions, and your old men shall dream dreams...*
> [21]*Then everyone who calls on the name of the Lord shall be saved.'*
> [22]*"You that are Israelites, listen to what I have to say: Jesus of Nazareth, a man attested to you by God with deeds of power, wonders, and signs that God did through him among you, as you yourselves know--*

Notice who Peter was addressing. What did he mean by "You that are Israelites"? Peter knew that the gathering of the House of Israel (the Lost Tribes) to God was to happen at the end time. As he understood conditions, he believed it WAS the end time.

However, much time would pass before the northern kingdom would come back. Instead, new developments took place within the sect.

Funk & Wagnall's New Encyclopedia (volume 15 *"Jews/ Christianity appears"*) describes this period of time that takes us from the synagogue to the church:

> *The last century of the ancient Jewish state was marked by religious and political upheaval. At the beginning of the Christian era the Jewish population in the ancient world numbered some 8 million living outside Judea, mainly in Alexandria, Cyrenaica (northern Africa), Babylon, Antioch, Ephesus, and Rome.*
>
> *This dispersion created, in addition to the force of Hellenism, several movements that struck at Judaism. One was directed against all Jews and took the form of anti-Jewishness based on business competition, religious difference, and the political privileges granted to many Jews who rose to high office. A second movement came from within Judaism itself, as Christianity.*
>
> *The Greek Jews who came to believe in Jesus (Heb. Yeshua, or Joshua) as the promised Messiah far outnumbered the Judeans who accepted Jesus. Moreover, as the disciples of Jesus traveled through the ancient world, many pagans were converted to the new belief. Christianity was originally regarded as a Jewish sect, but as more and more pagans were accepted into Christianity, their faith revolved almost entirely about the person and preaching of Jesus. The Judeo-Christians, on the other hand, remained, essentially, Jews. The Jewish answer to these new movements was to permit no laxity in observance of the forms of traditional religion.*
>
> *During the 1st century AD, religious conflict caused bloody battles. The Roman governors of Judea were despotic and gave little respect to the Jewish religion. In AD 66 a violent insurrection, led by the Zealots, a fanatic Jewish sect, began against Rome.*

Nero, then emperor, sent the Roman general Vespasian (later emperor) to put an end to the conflict. By 70 the revolt was crushed, the Temple was destroyed, and Jerusalem was razed; Masada, the last fortress, fell in 73.

Nominally, Judea continued to exist. The center of Jewish learning was transferred to Jabneh (Jamnia, now Yavne, Israel) under the direction of the great sage Johanan Ben Zakkai. For the next generation Judea was more or less peaceful, under strict Roman control. Then the Roman emperor Hadrian ordered Jerusalem rebuilt as a pagan city, to be called Aelia Capitolina, in honor of Jupiter; at the same time he issued an edict banning circumcision. This double insult caused consternation among the Jews of the Diaspora as well as those of Judea.

A violent revolt occurred in Judea, under Simon Bar Kokhba. From 132 to 135 the Jews made a desperate stand against the Roman legions and were, for a time, successful.

When the rebellion was finally put down by Rome, Judea was prostrate. By order of the emperor the very name of the province was discarded and changed to Syria Palaestina. Jerusalem was made a pagan city, and the death penalty was decreed for any Jew who entered its gates. Persecution of Jews became common throughout the empire.

Moreover, the fall of Judea created a greater rift between Jews and Christians. The Jews considered the loss a calamity, but the Christians saw it as a manifestation that God had abandoned the Jews and viewed themselves as the true bearers of divine grace. During the first three centuries of the Christian era, Christianity became increasingly powerful. After 313, when Constantine I emperor of Rome, accepted the new religion for himself and his empire, Christian antagonism against and, later, persecution of Jews became widespread.

Pagans, Pagans Everywhere

When Gentiles began to be accepted into the faith, it was like an explosion. The number of Gentile "believers" and the speed at which they "converted" were staggering. Remember, however, that these were not full converts to Judaism. You now had Gentiles accepting Yeshua as the Jewish messiah without even knowing or understanding the basic beliefs that Messiah was to promote.

Howard Vos in his book Exploring Church History writes:

> *Though Christianity was winning a victory of sorts over paganism, paganism achieved victories of her own by infiltrating the Christian church in numerous subtle ways. As opposition to paganism increased, many took their place in church without experiencing conversion. Thus large segments of church membership consisted merely of baptized pagans. The distinction between Christianity and paganism became increasingly blurred as the state church was established under the ultimate authority of the emperor.*

We need to remember that they were not JUST "brand new believers in Yeshua," they were ALSO brand new believers in the God of Abraham, Isaac and Jacob. Before this time they were PAGANS, worshiping OTHER gods!

Acts 17:22 RSV

> [22] *Then Paul stood in front of the Areopagus and said, "Athenians, I see how extremely religious you are in every way.*
> [23] *For as I went through the city and looked*

carefully at the objects of your worship, I found among them an altar with the inscription, 'To an unknown god.' What therefore you worship as unknown, this I proclaim to you.
[24]*The God who made the world and everything in it, he who is Lord of heaven and earth, does not live in shrines made by human hands,*
[25]*nor is he served by human hands, as though he needed anything, since he himself gives to all mortals life and breath and all things.*

From these verses we see something very important. Just as the Jews were ready for a Messiah, the Greeks were ready for and were looking for God. In fact they were looking so hard they had created gods for everything!

As ready as they were, however, to receive this new religion, they had no education or background on which to base their newly acquired faith. So they did what they knew, and viewed the worship of the God of Abraham the way that was natural and familiar to them.

In his book This Hebrew Lord, **John Shelby Spong** writes:

> *When I analyze the language, the concepts, the understandings, the meanings in traditional religious patterns today, I discover that they come to us not from our biblical Hebrew heritage at all; rather they are the direct outgrowth of the Neoplatonic roots of Greek philosophy.*
>
> *The Christian faith was born in a Hebrew context, serving a Hebrew Lord – a life-giving, life loving, whole, free man. But when this faith moved outward from the Hebrew world into the Mediterranean civilization, it inevitably confronted the dualistic mind of the Greek world. After that confrontation, Christianity was never the same.*

> *Dualism became the basic mental assumption through which the Christian faith was viewed. It was a gradual occurrence. All material things did not suddenly become evil; it was much more subtle than that. Slowly but surely the Hebrew view of the goodness of creation and the wholeness of life was forgotten, and Christianity bought Greek dualism, the inevitable result being what I now call the Grecianization of the gospel.*

Those who became the "Christian Fathers" were not educated in the Torah. They were educated in Greek philosophy. The debate did NOT center on how to interpret the Torah; rather, it centered on which Greek philosopher to follow. Because the Gentile had a totally different paradigm, the manner in which they viewed what the earliest followers had written led them to entirely different conclusions.

In his book Our Father Abraham, **Marvin Wilson** writes:

> *Platonism holds that there are two worlds: the visible, material world and the invisible, spiritual world. The visible or phenomenal world is in tension with the invisible or conceptual world. Because it is imperfect and a source of evil, the material world is inferior to that of the spiritual. In this view, the human soul originates in the heavenly realm, from which it fell into the realm of matter. Though human beings find themselves related to both of these worlds, they long for release from their physical bodies so that their true selves (their souls) might take flight back to the permanent world of the celestial and divine.*
>
> *Plato's view of the cosmos was then transposed to man. The body was a prison for the soul. The immortal soul -- pure spirit -- is incarcerated in a defective body of crumbling clay. Salvation comes at death, when*

the soul escapes the body and soars heavenward to the invisible realm of the pure and eternal spirit.

This had a widespread influence upon the history of Christian thought. "The most important fact in the history of Christian doctrine was that the father of Christian theology, Origen, was a Platonic philosopher at the school of Alexandria." -- Werner Jaeger, "The Greek Ideas of Immortality," Harvard Theological Review 52 (July, 1959): 146.

Unlike the Greeks, the Hebrews viewed the world as good. Though fallen and unredeemed, it was created by a God who designed it with humanity's best interests at heart. So, instead of fleeing from the world, human beings experienced God's fellowship, love, and saving activity in the historical order within the world.

Although most of the early "Church Fathers" came from a Greek background, some were even more extreme in their views. Marcion, who would eventually be labeled as a heretic, gives one a glimpse at the ideas that were being promoted during this early point in Christian history.

Dr. John Garr writes:

In the middle of the second century, the Hebrew foundations of Christian faith were attacked by the first great heresy that challenged the church. Some of the ideas of this heresy so permeated the church's corporate psyche that it has not yet fully recovered its spiritual and scriptural equilibrium.

Marcion, son of a bishop of Sinope in Pontus (there is some question about this) joined the Syrian Gnostic Credo in Rome in developing a dualistic view of sacred history which postulated the existence of two gods, the good and gracious God (Christ) and the Demiurge (Jehovah of the Jews). Marcion taught an

> *irreconcilable dualism between gospel and law, between Christianity and Judaism. The Demiurge and his religion were seen as harsh, severe, and unmerciful, and they were cast into Hades by Christ, the good God.*
>
> *Marcion invented a new canon of Holy Scripture which included only an abridged Gospel of Luke and ten of Paul's epistles, some of which he edited. He wrested the words of Jesus in Matthew 5:17 to declare, "I am not come to fulfill the law and the prophets, but to destroy them."*
>
> *In Marcion's view, Christianity had no connection whatever with the past, whether of the Jewish or the heathen world, but had fallen abruptly and magically from heaven. Jesus, too, was not born, nor did he die. His body was a phantom to reveal the good God, and his death was an illusion. This Christ was not the Messiah predicted in the Old Testament; he was a totally new and unforeseen manifestation of the good God of Greek dualism. Because the rest of the apostles were Judaizing corrupters of pure Christianity, Christ called Paul as the apostle to preach the truth of Marcion's extreme antinomianism and anti-Judaism.*

Marcion was the first one to create a "New" Testament. He believed that the "Old" Testament should be discarded, and his influence is with us to this day. How could this have happened? Didn't the Jewish believers try to guide and influence the Gentile "converts"? One reason for this "oversight" is that the great increase of Gentiles into the sect happened at the same time that Roman oppression was growing. Within a few short years most of the Jewish leaders of the sect were no longer around.

The Changing of the Guard

Fox's Book of Martyrs, The First Persecution, Under Nero, A.D. 67

> *This was the occasion of the first persecution; and the barbarities exercised on the Christians were such as even excited the commiseration of the Romans themselves.*
>
> *Nero even refined upon cruelty, and contrived all manner of punishments for the Christians that the most infernal imagination could design. In particular, he had some sewed up in skins of wild beasts, and then worried by dogs until they expired; and others dressed in shirts made stiff with wax, fixed to axletrees, and set on fire in his gardens, in order to illuminate them.*
>
> *This persecution was general throughout the whole Roman Empire; but it rather increased than diminished the spirit of Christianity. In the course of it, St. Paul and St. Peter were martyred. To their names may be added, Erastus, chamberlain of Corinth; Aristarchus, the Macedonian, and Trophimus, an Ephesian, converted by St. Paul, and fellow-laborer with him, Joseph, commonly called Barsabas, and Ananias, bishop of Damascus; each of the Seventy.*

The Death of the Jewish leaders

The following is a list of those Jewish leaders of the sect who were killed before the destruction of the Temple in Jerusalem, *most of them at the hands of the Romans or other pagans*:

> Banabas - dragged out of the city and burned, at Salamina in Cyprus, A.D. 64
>
> Mark - dragged to the stake at Alexandria, died on the way, A.D. 64

Paul - beheaded at Rome, A.D. 69

Andrew - crucified at Patras A.D. 70

Bartholomew - tortured, then flayed alive, and finally beheaded in Armenia, A.D.70

Thomas - cast into a furnace, and his side pierced with spears in Calamina, A.D. 70

Matthew - nailed to the ground and beheaded at Nad-Davar, A.D. 70

Simon Zelotes and his brother Judas Thadeus,

both slain, one crucified, and the other beaten to death with sticks, A.D. 70

Mathias - tied on a cross upon a rock, stoned, and then beheaded, A.D. 70

70 disciples of Yeshua, and several fellow travelers of the Apostles - slain, A.D. 70

The Second Persecution, Under Domitian, A.D. 81

The emperor Domitian, who was naturally inclined to cruelty, first slew his brother, and then raised the second persecution against the Christians. In his rage he put to death some of the Roman senators, some through malice; and others to confiscate their estates. He then commanded all the lineage of David be put to death.

Nicodemus, a benevolent Christian of some distinction, suffered at Rome, and Protasius and Gervasius were martyred at Milan.

Timothy was the celebrated disciple of Paul and bishop of Ephesus, where he zealously governed the Church until A.D. 97. At this period, as the pagans were about to celebrate a feast called Catagogion, Timothy, meeting the procession, severely reproved them for their ridiculous idolatry, which so exasperated the people that they fell upon him with their clubs, and beat him in so dreadful a manner that he expired of the bruises two days later.

The Third Persecution, Under Trajan, A.D. 108

> *Trajan being succeeded by Adrian, the latter continued this third persecution with as much severity as his predecessor. About this time Alexander, bishop of Rome, with his two deacons, were martyred; as were Quirinus and Hernes, with their families; Zenon, a Roman nobleman, and about ten thousand other Christians.*
>
> *At the martyrdom of Faustines and Jovita, brothers and citizens of Brescia, their torments were so many, and their patience so great, that Calocerius, a pagan, beholding them, was struck with admiration, and exclaimed in a kind of ecstasy, "Great is the God of the Christians!" for which he was apprehended, and suffered a similar fate.*

The Fourth Persecution, Under Marcus Aurelius Antoninus, A.D. 162

> *Polycarp, the venerable bishop of Smyrna, hearing that persons were seeking for him, escaped, but was discovered by a child. After feasting the guards who apprehended him, he desired an hour in prayer, which being allowed, he prayed with such fervency that his guards repented that they had been instrumental in taking him. He was, however, carried before the proconsul, condemned, and burnt in the market place.*

If we look at history, most of the persecution and martyrdom did NOT come from the Jews ... but from the Gentiles (Romans). Why is there no mention of the ROMAN persecution in the New Testament? Because that was so commonplace, it was assumed that everyone KNEW about THAT. Although there was an occasional lifting of the oppression, the Gentile (or Roman) rule was a constant reality.

By 70CE (AD), the Temple was destroyed, Jews were forced to flee Jerusalem, and most of the leadership (of the followers of Yeshua), were dead. Between 70CE (AD) and 90CE (AD) there is very little recorded history. However, when the record resumes, we see a very different group of people emerging as the leadership within this messianic movement. The emerging leadership was unfamiliar with and uneducated in the Torah. So they did what they knew; and they understood their beliefs through a different perspective: a Greek perspective.

Their misunderstanding of the faith was not surprising since most of them didn't have the privilege of owning a Torah scroll. What they DID have were copies of letters and testimonies written by certain Apostles. These letters and testimonies were never intended to be understood as "law," and yet that is exactly what happened. The body of letters and testimonies that became the "New Testament" were soon not only given equal status to that of the law and prophets, they eventually became more important; a reality that would have made the first followers of Yeshua shudder.

A significant amount of what was to become the "New Testament" was written by one person; the Apostle Paul.

Who was Paul

From any account **Paul was a controversial individual**. Although he is the person credited as being the architect of many of the doctrines of Christianity, he was not one of Yeshua's 12 chosen "apostles". Who was Paul anyway?

Saul of Tarsus

We are first introduced to the Apostle Paul as "**Saul of Tarsus**", a fierce opponent of "the Way". Saul (Paul) is there when Stephen is stoned, as a leader in opposing the new movement.

Then suddenly he shows up saying that he has had a change of heart.

And although he claimed to have had a vision on the road to Damascus that change his allegiances, many of the Jewish leaders never accepted his sincerity. Paul was not well respected nor trusted, he did not communicate well, and he was difficult to get along with.

Some of Paul's contemporary antagonists claim that he had no Pharisaic training or background; he was the son of a Gentile who converted to Judaism in Tarsus, came to Jerusalem when an adult, and connected himself to the High Priest. Upon failing to make any advances in the established faith, he broke ties and conspired to start a new religion.

This information is not considered to be factual history by any historian. Rather, it is second hand hearsay, basically "gossip". It does, however, give us some valuable insight into how others, at the time, felt about Paul.

In reality, we can tell from Paul's writings that he DOES have a background in both the law and Jewish traditions. It, however, is equally apparent that those who copied and translated his writings did not.

So when Paul refers to Israel (the Ten Tribes) having their eyes blinded and rejecting God, it was misunderstood as being Jews who's eyes were blinded for not recognizing Yeshua as Messiah and God. When Paul says that a Gentile is not required to be circumcised or in other ways adhere to the law of Moses, (a position held by ANY Jew, even today) it is misunderstood to mean that <u>Jews</u> should not be circumcised or observe the Mosaic law.

Acts 21:20

> *...They glorified the Lord and said to him, "You see, brother, how many thousands of Jews there are which believe; and they are all*

zealous of the law.

[21]*And* ***they are informed that you teach all the Jews which are among the Gentiles to forsake Moses, telling them not to circumcise their children, or live according to our customs****.*

[22]*What shall we do? The people will certainly hear that you have come,*

[23]*so do what we tell you.*

It is surprising how many people (EVEN TODAY) believe this same rumor; that Paul said circumcision and keeping the Mosaic law was unnecessary for someone who is Jewish. See what they instruct Paul to do.

There are four men with us who have made a vow.

[24]*Take these men, join in their purification rites, and pay their expenses, so that they can have their heads shaved.* ***Then everybody will know there is no truth in these reports*** *about you, but that you yourself are living in obedience to the law.*

But what about Gentiles?

[25]*As for the Gentile believers, we have written to them our decision that they should abstain from food sacrificed to idols, from blood, from the meat of strangled animals and from sexual immorality.*

The Gentiles were ONLY required to observe the seven Noahide laws. To learn more they were allowed to attend synagogue with the Jews.

Acts 15:21

[21]*For Moses has been preached in every city from the earliest times and is read in the synagogue on every Sabbath.*

Paul maintained that Jews should continue to be circumcised ...

Acts 16:1-3

> [1]*He came to Derbe and then to Lystra where a disciple named* ***Timothy*** *lived, whose mother was a Jewess and a believer, but whose father was a Greek.*
> [2]*The brothers at Lystra and Iconium spoke well of him.*
> [3]***Paul*** *wanted to take him along on the journey, so he* ***circumcised him*** *because of the Jews who lived in that area, for they all knew that his father was a Greek.*

Remember, since Timothy's mother was Jewish, so was he. Titus, however, was not. (Galatians 2:3)

> [3]*But* ***Titus*** *who was with me, being a Greek,* ***was not compelled to be circumcised****.*

As Paul continued to preach and write to the Gentiles, people continued to misunderstand exactly what he was saying. History tell us that not only the Jewish population misunderstood Paul, the Gentiles also were confused by Paul.

2 Peter 3:15

> [15]*...Paul also wrote you with the wisdom that God gave him.*
> [16]*He writes the same way in all his letters, speaking in them of these matters.* ***His letters*** *contain some things that* ***are hard to understand****, which ignorant and unstable people distort as they do the other scriptures to their own destruction.*

Not only was there friction concerning his writings, Paul also had problems with his traveling companions.

Acts 15:37

> [37]*Barnabas wanted to take John, also called Mark, with them,*
> [38]*but Paul did not think it was wise to take him, because he had deserted them in Pamphylia and had not continued with them in the work.*
> [39]***They had such a sharp disagreement*** *that they parted company. Barnabas took Mark and sailed for Cyprus,*
> [40]*but Paul chose Silas.*

Paul also was in conflict with the Roman authorities. At the end of the book of Acts we read about those who came to listen to Paul while he was under house arrest imposed by the government:

Acts 28:25

> [25]***They disagreed*** *among themselves and began to leave after Paul had made this final statement: "The holy spirit spoke the truth to your forefathers when he said through Isaiah the prophet:*
> [26]*Go to this people and say,* ***You will be ever hearing but never understanding****.*

Paul's life ended in 69CE. He was beheaded in Rome during a time of great upheaval; one year before the Temple was destroyed and the Jews were driven from Jerusalem.

The Split

Paul was a divider, not a uniter, and the followers of "the Way" divided into two groups; those "Jewish" followers known as Nazarenes or Ebionites, and the "Greek" followers who, years after Paul's death, emerged as the church fathers, founders of the universal or catholic church.

We can not be totally sure what started the separation from Gentiles on the Sabbath, but by 90CE the division was near complete. Observing the Sabbath seems to be completely removed from the practices of most Gentile "Christians".

Gentiles were discouraged from attending synagogue (as was suggested at the Jerusalem conference). Why would that be? There is a belief (even among many Jews today) that a Gentile SHOULDN'T study Torah or observe the Sabbath. That a Gentile is, in fact, required to BREAK the Sabbath.

Where does THAT belief come from? **Rabbi Moshe Kerr** explains:

> *Its a fundamental mistake in scholarship to confuse a secondary commentary for being a primary source! ...The Midrash gives a alligorical story that a non bnai brit which keeps Shabbot does not get a "reward". ...Now not getting a reward for doing a great mitzva and being put to death for doing a great mitzva seem poles apart. But in fact the midrash interprets the meaning of "death". A non bnai brit has no commandment to do commandments. ...Hence no reward means, even though they do commandments when their physical body dies, their soul dies.*

We are NOT considered righteous by the number of laws we keep. If a pagan observes the Sabbath or studies Torah (things that he is not required to do) while ignoring the seven Noahide laws, there is nothing "magical" about Sabbath observance to gain him a place in the World to Come. So if a pagan studies Torah or keeps the Sabbath he merits death (receives no reward), it however does NOT mean that he should be prohibited from doing so.

Gentiles would even bring their sacrifices to the Temple in Jerusalem. **Rabbi Elijah Benamozegh** writes:

> *In the Jewish doctrine relating to sacrifices, we find an implicit statement on the subject of the Noachides. It is the principle that sacrifices offered in the Temple by Gentiles ought to be accepted, whereas those brought by apostate Israelites must be refused. This obviously assumes that the mitzvot of the Mosaic Law are not binding upon Gentiles, for no special authorization would be needed for a practice which was not only a right but an obligation. When a Gentile offers such a sacrifice, he is observing part of the Law voluntarily. [Israel and Humanity p.246]*

What should have been Noahides worshiping <u>along side of Jews</u> in synagogues with the <u>same religious faith</u> (varying in personal obligations), became a totally new religion. We know from history that Sunday observance <u>among the Gentiles</u> was practiced almost from the beginning, and the belief that a Gentile SHOULDN'T keep the Sabbath may have been a contributing factor in this.

Soon Gentiles were meeting in their homes, and eventually set up "churches" as places of worship for the new faith. The first Christian church buildings appear early in the third century, and as the physical Christian houses of worship began to take a more dominant position in society, so did the new faith's political power.

In addition, Christianity became increasingly hostile toward Judaism. After the Jews were driven from Jerusalem, the Gentiles saw this as a sign from God that now THEY had become the chosen people, and the split became firm and permanent.

Christians also began to talk about "abolishing" the law.

Again, **Rabbi Benamozegh** writes:

> *It is not surprising that those Jews who while believing in Jesus, still did not intend to give up the Law for him, were alarmed by the conversion of that mass of pagans who, in their ever-increasing numbers, threatened to destroy Mosaism with the rallying cry of the new Christianity: "The Law is abolished!" [Israel and Humanity p.244]*

In time, "Christianity" became almost entirely Greek as the Jewish followers of "the Way" eventually ceased to exist.

In his book Early Christian Fathers **Cyril Richardson** writes:

> *Outside the New Testament writings, the earliest Christian document we possess is an anonymous letter of the church of Rome to the church of Corinth. It was written about AD 96.*
> *The most striking facts about early Christian literature are its rich variety and its almost exclusively Gentile authorship.* [pp 15]

Since the Gentiles were familiar with Greek philosophy and not with the Torah, they interpreted Paul's letters from a very different perspective.

The writings of Paul and others of his contemporaries also began to be considered to be as authoritative as the word of God (the Torah), after their death. The idea, originally proposed by Marcion, to create a "new" testament, also began to grow, and for the next couple of centuries became a political struggle as to what books were authentic, and whose version of a "new" testament would be used to shape the doctrinal direction of the Gentile believers who were already far from the Jewish perspective.

What About Peter?

One of the unspoken mysteries in Christianity is; What happened to Peter? It would seem that the Apostle Peter had been hand picked by Yeshua to be the leader of the new movement in Judaism.

Matthew 16:17

> *Blessed are you, Simon Barjona: for flesh and blood has not revealed it to you, but our Father which is in heaven.*
> *And I say to you, that you are Peter, and upon this rock, I will build my congregation.*

Peter was the one reported to have walked on water, and was the clear leader in the Gospel stories. But after Paul's emergence, Peter seems to have disappeared. Even at the Jerusalem conference (in about the year 50), Peter seems absent and James (Yeshua's brother) has emerged as the leader.

Catholic tradition names Peter as the first pope of the Catholic Church. Protestants, however, disagree and say that Peter was crucified upside-down in about the year 69. But a Jewish tradition says that Peter did not agree with the direction that the early Greek leaders were taking "Christianity" and he disassociated himself from the new religion.

The Rabbeinu Tam was reportedly a great admirer of the apostle Peter, claiming that he was:

> *"a devout and learned Jew who dedicated his life to guiding gentiles along the proper path"*

Rabbi Tam also gives Peter credit for writing the Nishmat prayer said in the morning service of the Sabbath and Festivals. According to this tradition, Peter remained a devout Jew and became totally separated from the "Christian" movement.

Whatever the case may be, as time went on the leadership of

"The Way" lost most all of their Jewish leaders and the Hebraic perspective diminished as pagan influences grew. The main body of believers was now moving firmly out of Judaism and into paganism.

By 325CE (AD), at the Council of Nicea, church leaders met to codify Christian doctrines, led by the Roman Emperor himself. Jewish bishops were specifically excluded from the meeting. It was decided that all Jewish customs must be discontinued and all Roman customs adopted. The council's intent was to forbid Christians to practice circumcision, Sabbath keeping, eating kosher, and to formally acknowledge the doctrine of the trinity. The concept of a triune Godhead was not universally accepted, and in some cases the bishops in attendance were threatened with death to achieve "agreement."

Observing customs that were considered to be "Jewish" had become illegal, and all subjects of the empire were mandated to accept this profession:

> *"I renounce all customs, rites, legalism, unleavened breads, and feast of Lambs of the Hebrews, sacrifices, prayers, aspirations, purifications, sanctifications, and propriations, hymns and chants, observances and synagogues, and the foods and drinks of the Hebrews. In one word, I renounce absolutely everything Jewish, every Law, rite and custom..." [Stefano Assemani, Acta Sanctorum Martyrum Orientalium at Occidentalium, Vol 1 (Rome 1748)] page 105.*

The customs and the culture of "Christianity" became those of the pagan society of the Roman Empire including the days that were honored as "holy"; now those of pagan deities rather than the Holy Days of God.

Chapter 7
Why Keep the Holy Days

I heard a radio commercial for a Christian bookstore promoting a sale they were having for Easter. The ad stated that Christians should celebrate the real meaning of Easter. I remember thinking how strange it would be if the listeners actually did what the commercial was asking them to do.

The original Easter was a holiday named after a fertility goddess. That is why rabbits and eggs are still associated with the holiday to this day. How did Christianity move from a religion that worshiped the One God to a religion that celebrates an ancient holiday that still bears the name of the pagan deity?

Just how much influence did Greek society have on the early church? In a Q & A column of Dr. James Dobson's "Focus on the Family" magazine he was asked the following question.

> **Q** *"Does our celebration of Christmas have some roots in pagan religious practices? How do you feel about Christians participating in that sort of thing?"*
>
> **A** *"It's true that the timing of our modern Christmas season coincides with that of an ancient Roman festival, the Saturnalia. There's even an historical connection between the two. In the fourth century, Emperor Constantine declared Christianity the official religion of the Roman Empire and outlawed all pagan religious practices.*
>
> *"But it seems Constantine also had a fair understanding of human nature and was something of a diplomat. He didn't want the public outcry that would be sure to result if he simply banned the Saturnalia. He declared that the festivities should*

continue from year to year, but be given a new meaning. The old pagan holiday was transformed into a celebration of the birth of Jesus Christ – the most important event in human history! In time, the old pagan associations faded and were eventually forgotten.

"Despite the secular origins of the Christmas holiday, I am not troubled by its celebration. I do understand why other believers are, and I respect their point of view. "To my mind, it's what you make of the event that counts – as the old Emperor seems to have understood so well.

"I seriously doubt that any of us today are in much danger of being lured into the worship of Roman deities. For us, a much more serious threat is posed by the gods of materialism and secularism, who have so successfully established themselves on what Constantine intended to be holy ground.

"But it doesn't have to be that way. For our family, Christmas has traditionally been one of the spiritual highlights of the year, as well as the focal point of many treasured memories. It is my opinion that this holy holiday can be the same for any family that chooses to make it so."

Dr. Dobson's response sounds reasonable enough; but we need to ask a few questions: What was the full context in which Christianity adopted these pagan holidays as their own, and how much influence have they had on our modern observance?

The Christmas Tree

In his book "How it Started," **Webb Garrison** writes:

Many countries claim the distinction of having launched the custom of erecting Christmas trees, but it may have begun independently in several parts of Europe. Ceremonial worship of trees in ancient pagan rites almost certainly led to the decoration of trees at the time of the winter solstice. [pp 52]

We read about this practice from the prophet Jeremiah in **Jeremiah 10:1**.

> [1] *Hear the word which the LORD speaks to you, O house of Israel:*
> [2] *Thus says the LORD, Learn not the way of the heathen, and be not dismayed at the signs of heaven; for the heathen are dismayed at them.*
> [3] *For the customs of the people are vain: for one cuts a tree out of the forest, the work of the hands of the workman, with the ax.*
> [4] *They deck it with silver and with gold; they fasten it with nails and with hammers, that it move not.*

Who made this a "holy day," and what days were replaced by these pagan observances?

December 25th

Again, **Webb Garrison** writes:

The festival of "Christes Masse"...was celebrated very early – at a variety of times and seasons. In AD 350 Pope Julius 1st formally designated December 25 as Christmas. He chose that date because it coincided with important pagan festivals. [pp 54]

From the book All About Christmas, **Maymie Krythe** writes:

A celebration at the time of the winter solstice, when all were looking forward to the coming of spring, was not an original idea with the Christians. For many years before Christ's birth, other religious groups had held festivals (connected with the earth's fertility) at the same season. The Romans, for example, observed the lavish Saturnalia – honoring Saturn, their god of agriculture – from the middle of December to the beginning of the new year. They exchanged gifts, and indulged in much eating, drinking, gaming, and visiting. Masked revelers on the streets often went to excess during this riotous celebration.

Since primitive peoples realized their dependence upon the sun as the source of light and life, sun worship was prevalent among them. In Persia at the winter solstice, they observed a notable feast to show their reverence for the sun, and they kindled great fires in homage on Mithra, their deity of light. Many of the Roman soldiers were adherents of Mithraism, a religion that for a time was a strong rival to Christianity in the Empire. Its most important feast day, Dies Solis Invicti Nati (Birth of the Unconquered Sun), occurred on December 25. [pp 1-3]

So we see that the adoption of this celebration into Christianity came about, not through a desire to more fully follow God's word and wishes, rather, it was through a purely political move to maintain control of the Empire.

In Exploring the New Testament World, **Albert A. Bell Jr.** writes:

Another eastern mystery cult, which proved enormously popular in Rome, especially among the army, was that of Persian Mithra. The cult first appeared in the eastern Mediterranean in the early first century B.C., when Rome was consolidating its control over the area. There is evidence that it reached Rome by about A.D. 80.

The cult grew so popular by the fourth century that it

seriously rivaled Christianity, especially among the business classes and the army, two segments of the population that the church had to win over if it was to consolidate its control of the empire. The mystery religions were nonexclusive. Initiates of one cult could join another, as long as they paid the fees and went through the rites. To judge from sermons that survive from this time, some Christians were also taking part in other cults, especially Mithra's.

One of the most popular aspects of Mithratic worship was the feast of the god, which fell on December 25, the day of his birth from a rock. According to Mithratic legend, shepherds brought gifts to the newborn god. It's worth noting also that the priests of this cult were called magi. [pp 140-141]

Where did the Mithra religion acquire its beliefs?

In Baptized Paganism, **Dennis Crews** writes:

Throughout history, the practice and horrors of sun worship have reached every region of the world. The Babylonians called the sun-god Shamash; the Egyptians, Ra; the Assyrians, Baal; the Canaanites, Moloch; the Persians, Mithras; the Greeks, Helios; the Druids, Hu; and the Romans, Sol Invictus--the Unconquerable Sun. The list continues down through history and encompasses cultures as diverse as the Hindus, the Japanese, and the Aztecs and comes as close to home as virtually every Indian tribe in North America. Most scholars trace the beginnings of sun worship to Babylon.

Nimrod & Semiramis

Babylon, the first metropolis, was founded by Nimrod soon after the flood (Genesis 10:8-10). Countless recitations of his mighty exploits elevated his status to superhuman proportions, and the rapidly expanding society at his feet finally began not only to honor him as their king, but to worship him as their god.

Nimrod's arrogance was ultimately surpassed only by that of his wife, Semiramis. Notoriously beautiful and cunning beyond imagination, she wielded her own power with an iron hand. Nimrod and Semiramis in their terrible strength and beauty were exalted as the sun and moon in human form.

Though historical accounts of Nimrod's actual death are vague, it is certain that he left Semiramis with a large dominion and an equally large dilemma. How was she to maintain her hold on the empire he had built? There was but one solution, and she pursued it with diabolical zeal. Nimrod's spirit had ascended into the sun itself, she claimed. With breathtaking eloquence she described to the people his new and elevated role as their benefactor and protector. Each morning he would rise, bringing light and life to the land as he traveled across the sky. In the evening he would plunge below the edge of the earth to battle the subterranean evil spirits and demons that would otherwise crawl over and annihilate mankind.

Tammuz and Ishtar

One spring not many years following Nimrod's death, the voluptuous Semiramis was found to be with child. Calling the scribes of Babylon together, she issued a most remarkable press release. Nimrod had impregnated her, she claimed, through the lively rays of the sun.

As the offspring of the sun-god, the anticipated child would itself lay claim to deity, and by proxy, she,

Semiramis, would henceforth be the "mother of god."

On December 25 Tammuz, the child of the sun-god, was born. His birth was hailed as a great miracle. Falling as it did during the slowly lengthening days immediately after the winter solstice; it was also seen as an omen of the sun's rebirth and was heralded by tumultuous rejoicing.

December 25 was thereafter observed as the birthday of the son of the sun-god, and became a yearly feast day throughout the kingdom.

Like his supposed father Nimrod, Tammuz was reputed to have been a great hunter. Perhaps his greatest conquest of all, however, was his mythical union with Ishtar, the mother goddess who embodied all the reproductive energies of nature. Also variously regarded as the moon goddess and the queen of heaven, Ishtar was the principal female deity of the Assyrians. This same goddess, with certain variations, can be identified in other cultures as Ashtoreth (Phoenecian), Astarte (Greek and Roman), Eostre (Teutonic), and Eastre (Saxon). Rabbits and eggs were both symbols of life and fecundity that early came to be identified with Ishtar. The yearly celebration honoring her took place around the first full moon after the spring equinox, when all of nature seemed to be bursting with reproductive vitality.

Unfortunately, the youthful Tammuz (also known as Adonis, meaning "lord," in classical mythology) met an untimely death at the tusk of a wild boar. Some accounts say that after three days Tammuz miraculously resurrected himself; others say that the grief-stricken Ishtar journeyed far into the nether-world to find him.

> *It may be unsettling to learn that virtually every religious holiday now observed throughout Christendom originated in paganism, many hundreds of years before Christ; but ancient history proves it beyond a doubt. [pp 3-5,7-10,12]*

There is not even a debate about the origins of the holidays celebrated by Christians today. They are not Biblical; and the specific dates have no historical significance connected with Yeshua. Should Christians continue to observe days that were adopted from paganism?

Deut. 12:29

> [29] *When the LORD your God shall cut off the nations from before you, where you go to possess them, and you succeed them, and dwell in their land;*
> [30] *Take heed to yourself that you be not snared by following them, after that they are destroyed from before you; and that you inquire not after their gods, saying, How did these nations serve their gods? even so will I do likewise.*
> [31] *You shall not do so unto the LORD your God: for every abomination to the* LORD, which he hates, have they done unto their gods; for even their sons and *their daughters they have burnt in the fire to their gods.*
> [32] *Whatever thing I command you, observe to do it: you shall not add to it, nor diminish from it.*

But if a Christian does not observe "Christian holidays," then which days should he observe? God gave the children of Israel the dates that He wanted them to observe in Leviticus 23. He did not change them. They are the ones that Yeshua himself observed; he was a Jew. They were the ones that the Apostles and first followers observed; they were all Jews.

Leviticus 23:1

> [1]*And the LORD spoke to Moses, saying,*
> [2]*Speak to the children of Israel, and say to them, Concerning the feasts of the LORD, which you shall proclaim to be holy convocations, these are my feasts.*

Strong's...

> **H4150** (feasts) mow'ed: an appointment, i.e. a fixed time or season.

Strong's...

> **H4744** (convocation) miqra': a public meeting, also a rehearsal

There are a few important points to notice here:

1) These are the feasts of God. They are not the feast of people.
2) The word, "mo-ed," means an appointed time. God is making an appointment; he is giving us the dates that he wants to meet with us.
3) They are to be public meetings where we gather with other people. And they are a rehearsal.

The first "feast day" that God tells us to observe is the Sabbath.

> [3]*Six days shall work be done: but the seventh day is the Sabbath of rest, a holy convocation; you shall do no work therein: it is the Sabbath of the LORD in all your dwellings.*

This is so important to God that he also includes this day as one of the Ten Commandments, which are listed in Exodus 20 and Deuteronomy 5. God ALSO puts emphasis on the Sabbath when giving Moses the two tablets of stone.

Exodus 31:13-18

> [13] *"Say to the Israelites, 'You must observe my Sabbaths. This will be a sign between me and you for the generations to come, so you may know that I am the LORD, who makes you holy.*
> [14] *"'Observe the Sabbath, because it is holy to you. Anyone who desecrates it must be put to death; whoever does any work on that day must be cut off from his people.*
> [15] *For six days, work is to be done, but the seventh day is a Sabbath of rest, holy to the LORD. Whoever does any work on the Sabbath day must be put to death.*
> [16] *The Israelites are to observe the Sabbath, celebrating it for the generations to come as a lasting covenant.*
> [17] *It will be a sign between me and the Israelites forever, for in six days the LORD made the heavens and the earth, and on the seventh day he abstained from work and rested.'"*
> [18] *When the LORD finished speaking to Moses on Mount Sinai, he gave him the two tablet's of the Testimony, the tablets of stone inscribed by the finger of God.*

Although Gentiles were never required to observe the Holy Days, anyone who was a "descendant of Jacob" (any Jew) was.

> 150AD JUSTIN: *...those who have persecuted and do persecute Christ, if they do not repent, shall not inherit anything on the holy mountain. But the Gentiles, who have believed on Him, and have repented of the sins which they have committed, they shall receive the inheritance along with the patriarchs and the prophets,*

and the just men who are descended from Jacob, even although they neither keep the Sabbath, nor are circumcised, nor observe the feasts. Assuredly they shall receive the holy inheritance of God. (Dialogue With Trypho the Jew, 150-165 AD, Ante-Nicene Fathers , vol. 1, page 207)

When did the observance of the Sabbath and the Biblical Holy Days stop, and worship on Sunday and the celebration of pagan deities begin? Much of the confusion began by people unfamiliar with the customs of those they were attempting to follow. Even today there are many Christians who believe that the Apostles and early followers of Yeshua met on "the first day of the week," or Sunday.

In the book Towards a Home Church Theology **Eric Svendsen** writes:

> *Luke records in Acts 20:7 "On the first day of the week we came together to break bread." Many who do not subscribe to NT patterns for church practice object to viewing Luke's words as normative for the church. Luke's words are purely narrative (it is argued) and do not have prescriptive force. Besides, this is the only place in Scripture that records the church meeting on Sunday. Even if we were to subscribe to NT patterns, one mention of meeting on Sunday does not constitute a pattern.*
>
> *In answer to this it must be admitted that this is indeed the only place in Scripture that expressly states that the church met together on Sunday. On the other hand, it must be stated with equal force that this is the only place in Scripture that specifically records on which day the early church met together.*

Is that true? What does the New Testament say about the Sabbath?

Sabbath in the New Testament

Yeshua and the Sabbath

Mark 1:21	*On the Sabbath he entered the Synagogue*
Mark 2:27	*The Sabbath was made for man, not man for the Sabbath*
Mark 6:2	*And when the Sabbath day was come, he began to teach in the Synagogue*
Luke 4:16	*As his custom was, he went into the Synagogue on the Sabbath day, stood up for to read.*
Luke 4:31	*Taught them on the Sabbath day*
Luke 6:6	*On another Sabbath, he entered the Synagogue and taught*
Luke 13:10	*And he was teaching in one of the synagogues on the Sabbath*
Luke 14:1	*As he went into the house of one of the chief Pharisees to eat bread on the Sabbath day*
Luke 23:56	*Rested on the Sabbath day according to the commandment*

The Apostles and the Sabbath

Acts 13:14	*They went into the Synagogue on the Sabbath day and sat down*
Acts 13:27	*Prophets read every Sabbath day*
Acts 13:42	*The Gentiles besought that these words might be preached to them the next Sabbath*
Acts 13:44	*And the next Sabbath day came almost the whole city*
Acts 15:21	*For Moses of old time has in every city them that preach him, being read in the Synagogue every Sabbath day*
Acts 17:2	*And Paul, as his manner was, went in unto them and three Sabbath days reasoned with them out of the scriptures*

Acts 18:4 *And he reasoned in the synagogue every Sabbath and persuaded the Jews and the Greeks*

Many well known, Sunday observing, scholars have commented on the Sabbath.

Peter K. Kraemer, Catholic Church Extension Society writes:

> *Regarding the change from the observance of the Jewish Sabbath to the Christian Sunday, I wish to draw your attention to the facts:*
>
> *1) That Protestants, who accept the Bible as the only rule of faith and religion, should by all means go back to the observance of the Sabbath. The fact that they do not, but on the contrary observe the Sunday, stultifies them in the eyes of every thinking man.*
>
> *2) We Catholics do not accept the Bible as the only rule of faith. Besides the Bible we have the living Church, the authority of the Church, as a rule to guide us. We say, this Church, instituted by Christ to teach and guide man through life, has the right to change the ceremonial laws of the Old Testament and hence, we accept her change of the Sabbath to Sunday. We frankly say, yes, the Church made this change, made this law, as she made many other laws, for instance, the Friday abstinence, the unmarried priesthood, the laws concerning mixed marriages, the regulation of Catholic marriages and a thousand other laws. It is always somewhat laughable to see the Protestant churches, in pulpit and legislation, demand the observance of Sunday, of which there is nothing in their Bible.*

It says in The Sunday Problem, a study book of the United Lutheran Church:

> *We have seen how gradually the impression of the*

Jewish Sabbath faded from the mind of the Christian Church, and how completely the newer thought underlying the observance of the first day took possession of the church. We have seen that the Christians of the first three centuries never confused one with the other, but for a time celebrated both.

Why is it that many Christians believe that the Sabbath has changed from Saturday to Sunday? One reason for this is not understanding the term "first day of the week." In a Hebraic culture, this would have been an awkward phrase. Instead of saying "first day of the week," you would have simply said "first day." If you were going to meet with someone on the "second day," you were probably not referring to a day two days later. Rather, you were saying, "Let's meet on the day we know today as 'Monday'."

Throughout the Bible you will NOWHERE find references to events that happened on the second day "of the week," third day "of the week," or any other day "of the week."

Then what is being talked about in the New Testament when it says "first day of the week"? If you are reading the King James Version of the Bible, you will notice that the word "day" is in italics. It will appear as "first *day* of the week." This means that the word "day" was added by translators to make the meaning more clear. What it should say is "on the first of the weeks." What is meant by the phrase "first of the weeks"?

During the Passover season, there is a day on which the wave sheaf offering is cut. This day begins the first of seven weeks of counting. The day after the counting of seven weeks is when Shavuot or the day of Pentecost falls. The barley harvest takes place during these seven weeks, but the harvesting cannot begin UNTIL the first sheaf of grain is offered to God. The day of the wave sheaf is "the first of the weeks." The places in the New Testament that say "first *day* of the week" are referring to this day.

Although the day of cutting the wave sheaf should be an important day to Christians (as should all of the Biblical Holy Days), the seventh day Sabbath remains the most important messianic observance.

Jewish tradition says that if all of Israel were to keep the Sabbath for just one day, then Messiah will come. Many Jews believe that the prophecy is talking about every single Jew keeping the Sabbath. That is not what is meant. It is the time that ALL ISRAEL -- BOTH HOUSES (the house of Judah AND the house of Israel) keep the Sabbath. There will always be secular Jews and secular Israelites, but when both houses of Israel come together and keep the Sabbath, Messiah will come.

If we look at the end-time prophecies we see why God is upset with the house of Israel.

Sabbath in Ezekiel

Ezekiel 20:12 *...gave them my Sabbaths to be a sign between me and them.*
Ezekiel 20:13 *...my Sabbaths they greatly polluted.*
Ezekiel 20:16 *...polluted my Sabbaths...*
Ezekiel 20:21 *...polluted my Sabbaths...*
Ezekiel 20:24 *...polluted my Sabbaths...*
Ezekiel 22:8 ...profaned my Sabbaths...
Ezekiel 22:26 *...hid their eyes from my Sabbaths...*
Ezekiel 23:38 *...profaned my Sabbaths...*

Notice that is says Sabbaths (plural). That means both the weekly and the annual Sabbaths.

Continuing again in **Leviticus 23:4**

> [4]*These are the feasts of the LORD, even holy convocations, which you shall proclaim in their seasons.*

In the following verses, we find the Biblical Holy Days listed.
1) The Passover in verse five.
2) The Days of Unleavened Bread in verses six through eight.
3) The Wavesheaf in verses 10 through 14.
4) The Counting of the Omer in verses 15 and 16.
5) The Day of Pentecost (or Shavuot) in verses 17 through 20.
6) Feast of Trumpets (Rosh Hashana) in verses 23 through 25.
7) The Day of Atonement (Yom Kippur) in verses 26 through 32.
8) The Feast of Tabernacles (Sukkot) in verses 33 through 36.
9) The Eighth Day in verse 36.

So, should Gentile Christians observe Jewish days?

Although at this time there does not appear to be any requirements on Gentiles to observe the Sabbath and the annual Holy Days, Ezekiel certainly says that those from the nation of "Israel" (both kingdoms) are expected to do so, and the prophet Zechariah writes about a time ALL nations are required to attend the fall Feast of Tabernacles (Sukkot).

Zechariah 14:16

> [16]*And it shall come to pass that everyone who is left of all the nations which came up against Jerusalem shall go up from year to year to worship the King, the LORD of hosts, and to keep the Feast of Tabernacles.*
> [17]*And it shall be that whichever of the families of the earth do not come up to Jerusalem to worship the King, the LORD of hosts, on them there shall be no rain.*

Elsewhere we see that the mixed multitude that came out of Egypt with the Israelites were supposed to observe the Sabbath (as long as they were with the Israelites).

Exodus 20:10

> *The seventh day is the Sabbath of the LORD your God. In it you shall do no work: you, nor your son, nor your daughter, nor your manservant, nor your maidservant, nor your cattle, nor the stranger who is within your gates.*

Yet, a Gentile was forbidden to eat the Passover lamb unless he WAS circumcised.

Exodus 12:43

> *... No outsider shall eat it. But every man's servant who is bought for money, when you have circumcised him, then he may eat it. A sojourner and a hired servant shall not eat it. ... When a stranger sojourns with you and wants to keep the Passover to the LORD, let all his males be circumcised, and then let him come near and keep it; and he shall be as a native of the land. For no uncircumcised person shall eat it.*

This may explain why Paul seems to institute a new observance, different from a traditional Passover seder, (1Cor. 11:17) for the Gentile believers.

A New Religion

As Christianity began to grow among the Gentiles, however, a new religion emerged. This was never the intention of the early followers of "the Way". What was NOT holy became holy, and what was holy lost it's holiness.

This leaves us with some hard questions to answer. If all Christians have the Bible as their sacred text, it would seem to follow that the days which are observed should be those found in the Bible rather than days created in honor of pagan deities.

It would also seem wise to not ONLY look into our observances, but also some of the basic themes and beliefs that developed early in Christian history. If Christian holidays come from paganism, where do basic beliefs like salvation come from?

Chapter 8
What is the Point of Salvation?

"Are you saved?" That was the questioned posed to me during a call-in show that I was hosting. I responded by asking, "What do you mean by that question?" The caller then quickly retorted, "If you have to ask, that just shows that you're not." So for the next hour I took phone calls from people: each with a different definition of "being saved."

How can that be? How can we have so many views on "being saved"? This seems like something that should be better defined, especially since many people will tell you the exact point in time that they became saved. What does salvation mean? Are there different ways to be saved? What is the point, the event, the place in time when you are saved? Is salvation a condition or a process? And how does a person "become saved"?

A "Personal" Savior

Many Christians can tell you the exact date and time that they "became saved." Many Christians believe that when you accept Jesus into your heart (or as your personal savior) then you are saved. But what does THAT mean? The main Christian perspective of salvation seems to be the necessity of knowing WHO the Messiah is. If this is true, how do we reconcile the Old Testament and the New Testament views of salvation? Does the accepting of, or having a knowledge of Messiah save us?

In the New Testament the message seems to be that those who believe or accept that Yeshua is their personal savior will be saved, while the Old Testament seems to be silent on the importance of knowing the Messiah's identity. Why is this? Why does the New Testament seem to stress belief in

Yeshua, and yet, nowhere in the entire Tanakh (Old Testament) do we even have a hint that salvation is tied directly with knowing WHO Messiah is? If the identity was so central to salvation, wouldn't there be more importance placed on knowing the Messiah's identity in the Tanakh?

When Yeshua was asked about eternal life he didn't stress the importance of knowing who the Messiah was, rather he stressed the importance of keeping the commandments.

Matthew 19:16-17

> [16]*And, behold, one came and said to him, Good Master, what good thing shall I do, that I may have eternal life?*
> [17]*And he said to him, "Why do you call me good? There is none good but one, that is, God: but if you will enter into life, keep the commandments."*

As we have discussed earlier, the commandments or "laws" are God's instructions for us. If we follow those instructions our lives will go better. If we do not follow God's instructions then we are "missing the mark," we are not on target.

The Hebrew word chata and the Greek word hamartia mean "to miss the mark." They are usually translated into the English word "sin." In the original language, to live your life "without sin" does not mean that you never make mistakes. Rather, it means that you are focused on the objective; you do not "miss the mark".

This is much like when the Bible says that Noah or Abraham were "perfect". The Bible is not telling us that Noah and Abraham never made a mistake.

John describes sin in **1John 3:4** this way:

> [4] ... *sin is transgression of the law*

Once Israel had been redeemed by God to be a "holy" or separated people, they were responsible to live a life free from "sin." Anyone who falls short, or "misses the mark," needs to be forgiven of those "sins."

Forgiveness of Our Sins

What exactly is the process by which our sins are forgiven?

In Israel during Temple times, there was a sacrificial system by which someone who had unintentionally sinned could be forgiven.

Leviticus 4:26

> [26]*And he shall burn all his fat upon the alter, as the fat of the sacrifice of peace offerings: and the priest shall make an atonement for him as concerning his sin, and it shall be forgiven him.*

But how does this match with what is written in **Hebrews 10:4**?

> [4]*It is not possible that the blood of bulls and goats should take away sins*

The writer of Hebrews knew the scriptures in the Torah that clearly state that when someone who had sinned brought a sacrifice to the Temple, his sins were forgiven. He, however, also knew that it was not the blood of an animal that forgave the sin, because if a person could not afford an animal sacrifice even a meal offering was sufficient.

There were also other ways to be "cleansed" from sin. One was to go into a ritual bath called a "mikvah." We read about this practice in the book of Mark.

Mark 1:4

> [4] *John did baptize in the wilderness, and preach the baptism of repentance for the remission of sins.*

[5] And there went out unto him all the land of Judea, and they of Jerusalem, and were all baptized of him in the river of Jordan, confessing their sins.

It is NOT, however, the ritual that saves a person. When a priest or John the Baptist would tell someone one that their sins were forgiven, it was not ultimately because of the ritual. No amount of sacrifice or ritual bathing is able to "save" someone without having a humble and giving attitude.

Hosea 6:6

[6] I desire mercy, and not sacrifice, and knowledge of God more than burnt offerings.

Psalm 34:18

[18] The LORD is near to them that are of a broken heart; and saves such as to be of a contrite spirit.

The main point to realize is that there is nothing magic about ritual baths or animal sacrifices. Although they may be part of a system or process, it is our heart and soul (our attitude) that make the difference.

Likewise "being saved" is not based solely on our experiences, feelings, or our acceptance of intellectual concepts.

Ultimately it is totally in God's hands. He may choose to save us in any fashion that He wishes, although the process is usually not without a certain amount of work and effort required.

The Saving Process

We also see evidence that "being saved" is not just a point in time; rather it is a process that takes us THROUGH a period of time.

Matthew 10:22

> [22]*And you shall be hated of all men for my name's sake: but he that* <u>*endures*</u> *to the end shall be saved.*

How does keeping the commandments and "enduring till the end" fit in with salvation? Also, how does that compare to other verses that indicate that our faith or belief is sufficient for salvation?

Believe, and You Shall Be Saved

One problem is that any time you translate from one language to another, you have to do a certain amount of interpretation. Although in our language the words "faith" or "belief" mean "to have a knowledge of," in the first century they meant more than that.

In **Edward Nydle's** <u>Beginner's Torah Lesson #6</u> he says:

> *To the average Believer "faith" is a mental activity that involves intellectual assent to the truth found in the Scriptures. It remains in the realm of the mind with no action attached to it. We say a prayer and you are "saved" by faith. This is NOT the Hebraic or Scriptural concept of belief. (Ya'akov-James 1:19-25; 2:12-26). We have allowed the Greeks to redefine our Scriptural words to fit their philosophy. Let us return to the Hebrew once again to obtain our word definitions and meanings with the Hebrew mind-set.*
>
> *The Hebrew verb AMAN means "faith, trust, believe, support, nourish, make firm or lasting." Notice it is a VERB. It is interesting that the Hebrew words OMENET (nurse) and OMENOT (pillars) come from this root. The Hebrew word –EMUNAH means "faithfulness, trust, firmness, stability, support, to be reliable." It is*

first used in Shemot (Exodus) 17:12 concerning Mosheh's hands being EMUNAH or steady or firm so the battle could be won over the Almalikites. This required an action on the part of Mosheh for deliverance to come to Yisrael.

So what does this mean; are we then saved by our own works? Absolutely not! In Romans, Paul says that we were saved while we were yet sinners. Just as the children of Israel did not receive salvation from Egypt because of any works that THEY did, rather God CHOSE them and redeemed them as a GIFT.

Salvation is not something that can be earned. However, after being saved we must live life in a saved condition, by following God's instructions (laws). In reality, being saved has more to do with living your life TODAY than it has to do with what will happen in an after-life.

But doesn't getting saved mean that you're going to heaven?

The Kingdom of "Heaven"

We read in the New Testament both John the Baptist and Yeshua saying, "Repent, for the kingdom of heaven is at hand."

Matt. 3:1

> [1]*In those days John the Baptist came, preaching in the wilderness of Judea,*
> [2]*And saying, Repent you, for the kingdom of heaven is at hand.*

Matt.4:17

> [17]*From that time Yeshua began to preach, and to say, Repent: for the kingdom of heaven is at hand.*

What does "the kingdom of heaven" mean? We find this phrase 40 times in the Bible. They are ALL in the book of Matthew. Why? Matthew is the most Hebraic of the Gospels. He was careful to not over-use God's name.

So rather than say "kingdom of God" (like all of the other Gospels), he would replace the name of God with "heaven." This was not to say that this kingdom's physical location was IN heaven. Rather, this was the kingdom that was serving as a representative OF heaven or God.

It is easy to misunderstand what is being said because we often do not understand the culture or context, and because we are working through translation and interpretation difficulties.

When Yeshua said that the kingdom of God was "not of this world," did he mean that it was up in heaven? In Hebrew the word "olam" is sometimes translated as "world." In Jewish theology the present age is the Olam Hazeh. The Olam Haba is "the World to Come."

The World to Come is not that of a different planet someplace, nor is it one of floating on clouds up in heaven. It is a belief in an AGE to come, here on this planet, when Messiah will rule. So the kingdom of God will be in an age to come.

But isn't the gospel the story of salvation through Yeshua?

The Gospel

If you were to ask the average Christian what the gospel was, he would probably say it was Jesus dying for our sins so we can go to heaven when we die. But, is that really what the "gospel" is all about? What is the gospel anyway?

The word "gospel" means "good news." What was the "good news" about?

Matthew 4:23

> *And Yeshua went about all Galilee, teaching in their synagogues, and preaching the gospel of the kingdom, and healing all manner of sickness and all manner of disease among the people.*

Matthew 9:35

> *And Yeshua went about all the cities and villages, teaching in their synagogues, and preaching the gospel of the kingdom, and healing every sickness and every disease among the people.*

Matthew 24:14

> *And this gospel of the kingdom shall be preached in all the world for a witness unto all nations; and then shall the end come.*

Mark 1:14

> *Now after that John was put in prison, Yeshua came into Galilee, preaching the gospel of the kingdom of God,*

Mark 1:15

> *And saying, The time is fulfilled, and the kingdom of God is at hand: repent you, and believe the gospel.*

Let us put the phrase, "kingdom of God," into context. What did that mean to people in the first century? In modern language we might say, the "nation" of God. Is there a nation that is "of God"? Is there a nation that God has chosen?

When salvation came to Israel

Both Houses of Israel received salvation from Egypt. This was both physical salvation from slavery and spiritual salvation.

Exodus 15:2

> [2]*The LORD is my strength and might, and he has become my salvation: he is my God, and I will glorify him; the God of my father, and I will exalt him.*

Deuteronomy 7:6

> [6] *You are a holy people to the LORD your God: the LORD your God has chosen you to be a special people to himself, above all people that are on the face of the earth.*

National Salvation

At Mount Sinai, God sanctified the entire nation of Israel as his chosen people. Christians can understand a personal and individual salvation, but a NATIONAL salvation is a much harder concept to grasp. In fact, that does not even seem possible. And yet that is what we see happening with the children of Israel.

God redeemed the nation of Israel out from slavery in Egypt, not because they were such a good and obedient people. But, while they were still in slavery (sin) God redeemed them, saving them from death through putting the blood of a lamb on their doorposts, and now, as a purchased people, they were expected to be obedient to God's instructions, (law).

By being obedient to God and striving to observe everything that God has told them, they are not EARNING salvation. Rather, they are obligated to follow God's instructions because they ARE a saved and chosen people.

Deuteronomy 14:2

> [2] *For you are a holy people unto the LORD your God; the LORD your God has chosen you to be a peculiar people unto himself, above all people unto himself, above all the nations that are upon the earth.*

It is curious that many Christians believe that a Jew is trying to achieve salvation through works, and that a Jew's attempt to keep the law is evidence of that. Nothing could be further from the truth.

What Does Salvation Mean?

The point of salvation for a Jew is the deliverance, as a nation, from slavery in Egypt. Not because of anything that they had done, but because of God's great mercy.

Salvation is a Gift from God. It does not depend on how good WE are. No amount of law-keeping can save us. However, once we ARE saved, it DOES matter how good we are, and obeying God's laws are extremely important, because we do not have a condition of "once saved, always saved." We CAN lose our salvation. There is a parable told by Yeshua in the book of Matthew that illustrates that point.

Losing Salvation

Matthew 18:23

> [23]*...The kingdom of Heaven is like a certain king, which would take account of his servants.*
> [24]*And when he had begun to reckon, one was brought to him, which owed him ten thousand talents.*
> [25]*But forasmuch as he had nothing to pay, his lord commanded him to be sold, and his wife, and children, and payment to be made.*
> [26]*The servant therefore fell down, and worshiped him, saying, Lord, have patience with me, and I will pay you all.*
> [27]*The lord of that servant was moved with compassion, and let him go, and forgave him his debt.*
> [28]*But the same servant went out and found one of his fellow servants, which owed him an hundred pence: and he laid hands on him, and took [him] by the throat, saying. Pay me what you owe me.*

[29]And his fellow servant fell down at his feet, and besought him, saying, "Have patience with me, and I will pay you all."
[30]And he would not; but went and cast him into prison, till he should pay the debt.
[31]So when his fellow servants saw what was done, they were very sorry, and came and told their lord all that was done.
[32]Then the lord, after he called him, said to him "O you wicked servant, I forgave you all that debt, because you wanted me to.
[33]Shouldn't you also have had compassion on your fellow servant, even as I had pity on you?"
[34]And his lord was angry, and sent him to prison, till he paid all that he owed.
[35]So likewise shall my heavenly Father do also to you, if you from your hearts do not forgive your brothers trespasses.

Once God gives you a gift, retention is not a guarantee. We know that King David prayed that God would not take His spirit from him (as had happened with King Saul). King David did not take for granted God's gifts to him. So once God has saved us from the penalty of sin, (which is death), and has given us the GIFT of eternal life in the "World to Come," we have an obligation of obedience to God. We must not take for granted what God has given us. Yet, that is exactly what Israel did, beginning with King David's son Solomon.

1 Kings 11:11

[11]So the Lord said to Solomon, since this is your attitude, and you have not kept my covenant and my decrees, which I commanded you, I will most certainly tear the kingdom away from you and give it to your servant.

As we read earlier, God split the kingdom in two and caused most of the children of Israel to go into captivity, losing their identity until the end of the age.

Isaiah 1:3-9

> [3] *The ox knows his owner, and the ass his master's crib: but Israel does not know, my people do not consider.*
> [4] *Ah sinful nation, a people laden with iniquity, a seed of evildoers, children that are corrupters: they have forsaken the LORD, they have provoked the Holy One of Israel to anger, they are gone away backward.*
> [5] *Why should you be stricken any more? you will revolt more and more: the whole head is sick, and the whole heart faint.*
> [6] *From the sole of the foot even to the head there is no soundness in it; but wounds, and bruises, and putrefying sores: they have not been closed, neither bound up, neither mollified with ointment.*
> [7] *Your country is desolate, your cities are burned with fire: your land, strangers devour it in your presence, and it is desolate, as overthrown by strangers.*

Israel was taken into captivity, and another people (later known as the Samaritans) were brought in by the Assyrians as replacements. The smaller kingdom in the south, however, retained its identity and salvation from God.

> [8] *And the daughter of Zion is left as a cottage in a vineyard, as a lodge in a garden of cucumbers, as a besieged city.*
> [9] *Except the LORD of hosts had left unto us a very small remnant, we should have been as Sodom, and we should have been like unto Gomorrah.*

In the book of Hosea, the prophet tells us that because Judah would retain the knowledge of God, they would be saved; but because Israel lost the knowledge of God the House of Israel would be destroyed.

Hosea 1:7

> *But I will have mercy upon the house of Judah, and will save them by the LORD their God, and will not save them by bow, nor by sword, nor by battle, by horses, nor by horsemen.*

Hosea 4:6

> [6]*My people are destroyed for lack of knowledge. Because you have rejected knowledge, I will also reject you from serving in my priesthood. Because you have forgotten the Torah of your God, I will also forget your children.*

It was the House of Israel that was cut off while the House of Judah was saved. Yeshua himself acknowledges this when talking to a Samaritan woman at a Jacob's Well.

John 4:22

> [22]*...we know what we worship, for salvation is of the Jews.*

It is through the faithfulness of the remnant of Israel (Judah, the southern kingdom) that Messiah will come and the House of Israel (the northern kingdom) will be saved. But how do you begin to find a people that have disappeared from history, let alone save them?

There has been much speculation over the passing of history as to where the northern kingdom has gone. Has it already returned? If so, WHERE is Messiah?

Before we answer that question, we must ask an even more important question: WHAT is Messiah?

Chapter 9
What is Messiah?

Jewish Messiah or Christian God?

Many Christians do not understand that the major difference between Christian and Jew is not a question of WHO Messiah is, rather it is a question of WHAT Messiah is. When we ask a Jew to "accept Jesus" we are not asking them to accept the Jewish Messiah, rather we are asking them to accept the Christian God.

Aime Palliere in his book "The Unknown Sanctuary" quotes **M. Loyson** as saying:

> *The chief reason why the Jews do not accept Christianity is that the latter departed from its origins in creating a God of secondary importance, as Justin Martyr said. And little by little after having made Jesus equal to the Heavenly Father, have we not practically substituted him for the Heavenly Father?*

How can believing that Jesus is God be "departing from our origins?" Isn't that what the founders of Christianity believed?

In his book <u>This Hebrew Lord</u>, **John Shelby Spong** writes:

> *The simplistic suggestion that Jesus is God is nowhere made in the biblical story. Nowhere!*

How can THAT be? If the first followers of Yeshua (who were all Jewish) did not believe that the Messiah was God, what DID they believe? And why is it that Christian and Jew have such different views on WHAT Messiah is? If this is the fundamental difference between us, it would make sense to explore the Jewish concept of Messiah, and discover WHEN and WHY the view of the divinity of the Messiah became different in Christianity. Again, we must ask the question: did the original believers have the same concept of the Messiah as do modern Christians?

The Jewish Perspective

The Shema is sometimes called the "Jewish Profession of Faith" because it begins with the most basic of Jewish concepts: "Hear O Israel, The LORD our God the LORD is One." In Judaism, Messiah is never confused with God, and is NEVER believed to be God.

In the New Testament accounts of the first believers, you will find much disagreement over the question of the association and conversion of Gentiles. You will find discussion of and disagreements over many other issues. However, there is no debate over the deity of Yeshua. Why?

The reason for this obvious absence of discussion on the topic is that this was not yet the view held by early believers. Had the belief of the early followers included the deity of Yeshua, the pages of the New Testament would be filled with the stories of conflict over such beliefs. The early followers historically did not take the position that the Messiah was God. If that is the case, WHO and WHAT is Messiah?

The Meaning of "Messiah"

The Hebrew word "Mashiach" means "anointed one" (or chosen one).

HEBREW	GREEK	ENGLISH
Mashiach (Messiah)	Christos (Christ)	Anointed

This title applies to the High Priest, to the Kings of Israel, and even to Israel itself.

In his book Early Judaism, **Martin Jaffee** writes:

> *The English word "Messiah" renders the Hebrew "mashiakh." In it's simplest meaning, it denotes "one who is anointed with oil." More expansively, it identifies a person consecrated to a divinely appointed task. In the Torah of Moses, particularly in the book of Leviticus, this term is used frequently to describe Aaron, the officiating priest charged with conducting the sacrificial service in the Tent of Meeting.*
>
> *In the priestly sense, the Messiah is the priest whose sacrificial service in accordance with Torah sustains the covenantal relationship between God and Israel. Messiah also refers to one anointed to serve as king over the Israelite people in its Land. The original anointee was Saul, the first man appointed as king over Israel.*

1 Samuel 24:5

> [5]*And it came to pass afterward, that David's heart smote him, because he had cut off Saul's skirt.*
> [6]*And he said unto his men, The LORD forbid that I should do this thing unto my master, the LORD'S anointed, to stretch forth mine hand against him, seeing he is the anointed of the LORD.*
> [7]*So David stayed his servants with these words, and suffered them not to rise against Saul. But Saul rose up out of the cave, and went on his way.*

Here we read of David referring to Saul as למשיח יהוה (or "the Messiah of the LORD"). So, there can be a number of different individuals identified throughout history as a messiah (anointed). However, when you talk of THE Messiah you would be referring to Messiah ben David, the ruler at the end of the age at the time of the Third Temple.

The Divine Connection

When answering the question WHO or WHAT is the Messiah, it is helpful to read what God tells Moses about the divine connection to Messiah.

In **Deuteronomy 18:18** God tells Moses:

> [18]*I will raise up a prophet from among their countrymen like you, and I will put My words in his mouth, and he shall speak to them all that I command him. And it shall come about that whosoever will not listen to My words which he shall speak in My name, I Myself will require it of him.*

As we can see, the Messiah was to be "from among their countrymen" like Moses. The connection to the divine is that God's WORDS are put in Messiah's mouth. It is important to realize that at no time in history did Judaism ever assign deity to the Messiah himself.

James D.G. Dunn in his book Christology in the Making writes:

> *...there is little or no good evidence from the period prior to Christianity's beginnings that the Ancient Near East seriously entertained the idea of a god or son of god descending from heaven to become a human being in order to bring men salvation, except perhaps at the level of popular pagan superstition. [p22]*

Why then did Christianity view Messiah as God?

The Gentile Factor

Remember that after 70CE (AD) the leadership within the "Christian" movement became dominated by Gentiles, who had formerly worshiped other gods.

Funk & Wagnalls New Encyclopedia *(volume 6 / Christianity)*

The Beginnings of the Church

> *An important source of the alienation of Christianity from its Jewish roots was the change in the membership of the church that took place by the end of the 2nd century (just when, and how, is uncertain). At some point, Christians with Gentile backgrounds began to outnumber Jewish Christians.*

The Gentile or Greek culture was centered around philosophy and mythology. Their entire perspective was that of having multiple gods. To them the most natural assumption was that messiah was a god. This, however, was NOT the perspective that the first century JEWISH population had (which included ALL of Yeshua's disciples).

But what about all of the passages like John 1 that also say Jesus is God. Remember, that much of our interpretation of scripture is from the perspective of those early "church fathers" who by the 2nd century were comprised of mostly Gentiles well educated in Greek philosophy.

In A History of God, **Karen Armstrong** writes:

> *Like the divine Wisdom, the "Word" symbolized God's original plan for creation. When Paul and John spoke about Jesus as though he had some kind of preexistent life, they were not suggesting that he was a second divine "person" in the later Trinitarian sense. They were indicating that Jesus had transcended temporal and individual modes of existence. Because the "power" and "wisdom" that he represented were activities that derived from God, he had in some way*

expressed "what was there from the beginning." These ideas were comprehensible in a strictly Jewish context, though later Christians with Greek background would interpret them differently. In the Acts of the Apostles, written as late as 100 CE, we can see that the first Christians still had an entirely Jewish conception of God.

Again, **Martin Jaffee** writes:

> *The canonical book of Proverbs portrays wisdom as being God's companion from the beginning of time. The image was refracted throughout the worlds of ancient Judaism. It informed many of Philo's descriptions of Torah as a divine logos (word, principle) through which Being conceived the world into existence. All that exists is as it should be because the world's structure is undergirded by divine thought, Torah.*

By the second century the leadership of Christianity had shifted from a Jewish majority (well educated in the Torah), to a Greek majority (well educated in Greek culture, philosophy and mythology).

As the Jewish sect began to be more dominated by a Greek membership, however, the Greek polytheistic perspective of God also became a more accepted view.

The Encyclopedia Britannica says:

> *The Trinitarians and the Unitarians continued to confront each other, the latter at the beginning of the third century still forming the large majority.*

In the course of time, those who believed that Messiah was God changed the intentions of it's original founders and alienated all Jewish participation. As Rabbi Yakov Fogelman writes:

> *Had the followers of Christ not insisted on his divinity, then the Jews might indeed have embraced Jesus as a Jewish revolutionary, who fought to remove Rome's oppressive hand*

from his people, and was murdered by Pontius Pilate for his act of rebellion against the mighty and intolerant authority of Rome. Jews might have embraced Jesus as another learned teacher who offered beautiful and stirring ethical lessons. They might have embraced Jesus as the man, who not only did not abrogate the Torah, but, said in Matthew, that anyone that gives up even a single letter of the law of Moses would be the least in the kingdom of heaven. But what the Jews could not, dare not, and indeed never will, accept is that Jesus was anything more than a mortal man.

A Change of Text

If we look at how the text of John 1:1 has changed over the years we can get a sense of how "clarifying" the text has helped to institutionalize the orthodox Christian doctrines.

First let's take a look at the **Tyndale Bible** of **1525**

> *"In the beginnynge was that worde, and that worde was with God: and God was that worde. The same was in the beginnynge with God. All thinges were made by it, and without it, was made nothinge, that made was. In it was lyfe; And lyfe was the lyght of men ..."*

As you can see, the Tyndale Bible of 1525 translates the word not as a person, but as God's speaking the world into existence. The word "word" (or worde) is not capitalized and it is referred to as an "it" and not a "he". Within a hundred years, however, the standard interpretation had changed.

We read the same passage in the **King James Version** (originally translated in **1611**)

> *"In the beginning was the Word, and the Word was with God, and the Word was God. All*

> *things were made by him; and without him was not any thing made that was made. In him was life; and the life was the light of men."*

This version of the Christian Bible "clarified" John 1:1. "Word" is now capitalized and referred to as a "he" instead of an "it". As future versions were written, more "clarifications" were made.

The **1971 Living Bible** reads as follows:

> *"Before anything else existed, there was Christ with God. He has always been alive and is himself God. He created everything there is -- nothing exists that he didn't make. Eternal life is in him, and this life gives light to all mankind."* (40 million sold by 1997)

Corruption of Scripture

The altering of texts did not begin, however, in the 1500's, **St. Faustus**, a 5th century Bishop writes:

> *"Many things have been inserted by our ancestors into the speeches of our Lord which, though put forth under his name, agree not with his faith; especially since, as already it has been often proved - these things were written not by Christ, nor [by] his apostles, but a long while after their deaths"*

As church orthodoxy began to develop through the second and third centuries the documents which would make up the New Testament were revised in order to establish the orthodox view. It was the Christological debates of the second and third centuries that finally led to the formation of the doctrine of the Trinity.

Bart Ehrman documents many of these revisions in his book <u>The Orthodox Corruption of Scripture</u>.

Ehrman writes:

> *Orthodox scribes not infrequently altered texts that might be taken to suggest that Jesus became the Son of God only at his baptism (Luke 3:22; Acts 10:37, 38; John 1:34), or at his resurrection (Rom 1:4), or at some unspecified moment (e.g., Luke 9:35; 1John 5:18). Correspondingly they changed other passages so as to highlight their view that Jesus was already the Son of God before his baptism (Mark 1:1) or even before his coming into the world (Matt 1:18).*
>
> *By far the most common anti-adoptionist corruptions simply designate Christ as "God."*

Here are a few examples of changes that were made to the text:

Corrupt Text	Original Text
Matthew 1:18 Now the **birth** of Jesus Christ happened this way:	Matthew 1:18 Now the **beginning** of Jesus Christ happened this way:
Luke 2:33 And **Joseph and his mother** marveled at those things which were spoken of him.	Luke 2:33 And **his father and mother** marveled at those things which were spoken of him.
Luke 9:35 And there came a voice out of the cloud, saying, **This is my beloved Son**: hear him.	Luke 9:35 And there came a voice out of the cloud, saying, **This is my son, the one who is chosen**: hear him.
John 1:34 And I saw, and bare record that this is the **Son of God**.	John 1:34 And I saw, and bare record that this is the **chosen of God**.

1 Timothy 3:16 And without controversy, great is the mystery of godliness: <u>**God was manifest in the flesh**</u>,	1 Timothy 3:16 And without controversy, great is the mystery of godliness: <u>**who was manifest in the flesh**</u>,

Ehrman goes on to say:

> *Finally, the orthodox emphasis on Jesus' divinity occasionally led to a de-emphasis on his humanity. So far as we can judge, scribes never eliminated the notion that Jesus was fully human. This would have embroiled them in a different set of problems, for then the text could be taken to support docetic Christologies that the proto-orthodox opposed on another front.*
>
> *But scribes did modify texts that could implicate Christ in human weaknesses and frailties that were not appropriate to one understood to be divine, occasionally changing passages that suggest that Christ was not all-knowing (Matt 24:36) or spiritually perfect (Luke 2:40), and passages that suggest that he was purely mortal (John 19:5) or susceptible to human temptations and sin (Heb 2:18; 10:29).*

The "Antichrist"

As time went on, the leadership of "the Way" became almost entirely Greek. Those who were Jewish or Hebraic were marginalized and labeled as heretics. As opposition to the Greek viewpoint diminished, there was a tremendous effort by the early Gentile "church fathers" to establish Jesus as God, and by the time his last living disciple, John, was in his old age (around 90CE) the idea of Yeshua as a divine being had already begun to become accepted among many Greek "Christians".

This is a doctrine that John calls "not messiah" or "Antichrist".

1 John 4:1

> [1]*Beloved, don't believe every spirit, but try the spirits to see if they are of God: because many false prophets are gone out into the world.*
>
> [2]*This is how you know the Spirit of God: Every spirit that confesses that Yeshua Messiah has come in the flesh is of God:*
>
> [3]*And every spirit that confesses that Yeshua Messiah has not come in the flesh is not of God: and this is that spirit of antichrist, that you have heard should come; and even now already is it in the world.*

By making messiah into a god, the Greeks were effectively making messiah into the opposite of what he was suppose to be.

John warned the people of his time not to turn from their Jewish roots. Not to make Yeshua into God.

2 John 1:6

> [6]*And this is love, that we walk after his commandments. This is the commandment, That, as you have heard from the beginning, you should walk in it.*
> [7]*For many deceivers are entered into the world, who confess not that Yeshua Messiah is come in the flesh. This is a deceiver and an* ***antichrist****.*
> [8]*Look to yourselves, that we lose not those things which we have wrought, but that we receive a full reward.*

The role of messiah is one who brings Israel OUT of idolatry and back to the worship of the One God. In essence, the belief in "Jesus" (the mainstream Christian view of who and what he was) is a belief that goes AGAINST what the role of messiah is. It is an anti-messiah (or antichrist) belief.

Yet John saw this belief grow stronger

1 John 2:18

> *Little children, it is the last time: and as you have heard that* ***antichrist*** *shall come, even now are there many antichrists; whereby we know that it is the last time...*
>
> *I have not written to you because you know not the truth, but because you know it, and that no lie is of the truth.*

In Jewish belief, the "son of God" is NOT "God the son". Messiah has never been confused with God. He has NEVER been considered a deity.

John believed that Yeshua was the messiah.

> *Who is a liar but he that denies that Yeshua is the Messiah?*

However, he believed that by making Yeshua into a god (and not distinguishing between God and Messiah), those who did such a thing were proposing a belief that was an insult to Jewish concept and tradition of what messiah was to be.

> *He is* ***antichrist****, that denies the Father and the Son.*
>
> *Whosoever denies the Son, the same has not the Father: [(but) he that acknowledges the Son has the Father also].*

John then appeals to his followers to abide by the Jewish traditions that they had heard "from the beginning".

> *Let that therefore abide in you, which you have heard from the beginning. If that which you have heard from the beginning shall*

remain in you, you also shall continue in the Son, and in the Father.

And this is the promise that he has promised us, [even] eternal life.

John anticipated the messianic age, the resurrection of the dead, and the "world to come" were all at the doorstep. He was unaware that there was to be two thousand years to follow.

In time, what had been the majority view became the minority view. Eventually, through creeds, various church councils, and the formation of Christianity as a state religion, the divinity of Messiah became the official church doctrine.

Funk & Wagnalls New Encyclopedia (volume 6 / Christianity)

Councils and Creeds

Early creeds began the process of specifying the divine in Christ, both in relation to the divine in the Father and in relation to the human in Christ. The definitive formulations of these relations came in a series of official church councils during the 4th and 5th centuries – notably the one at Nicaea in 325 and the one at Chalcedon in 451 – which stated the doctrines of the Trinity and of the two natures of Christ in the form still accepted by most Christians.

To arrive at these formulations, Christianity had to refine its thought and language, creating in the process a philosophical theology, both in Greek and in Latin, that was to be the dominant intellectual system of Europe for more than a thousand years.

Belief in a triune Godhead became the only accepted view of the nature of God. Anyone who believed otherwise would be put to death. Although there have been those throughout history that have not viewed the orthodox Trinitarian position as correct. In his article *Cosmic Codebreaker, Pious Heretic*, about Sir Isaac Newton (for Christian History Magazine), **Karl Giberson** writes:

> *Newton began a sustained reflection on the Christian doctrines and decided that the Anglican status quo was a thorough corruption of the true, original Christianity. These considerations led him to write over a million words on theology and biblical studies – more than he wrote on any other subject.*
>
> *Newton's theological investigations convinced him that the doctrine of the Trinity was bogus, a successful deception by St. Athanasius in the fourth century. Newton argued that the Scriptures had been altered and early Christian writers had been misquoted to make it appear that Trinitarianism had been the original faith.*

Newton believed that the scriptures had been altered. This was not just a statement of desperation. Rather, there was substance to his claims.

Giberson continues:

> *He [Newton] became repelled by what he perceived as the false religion that surrounded him – an idolatrous faith that worshiped Christ as God, when he was but a mediator between God and man.*

Newton was forced to keep his views at least partially veiled. The Unitarian position, (belief in the One God), however, began to make certain advances in the American colonies. Such notable people as Benjamin Franklin and Thomas Jefferson were Unitarian. Jefferson, himself, refers to Trinity as:

> *"...an unintelligible proposition of Platonic mysticism that three are one, and one is three; and yet one is not three and three are not one." "I never had sense enough to comprehend the Trinity, and it appeared to me that comprehension must precede assent."*

Jefferson further believes that the "One God" movement would sweep the nation if it was given the religious freedom the founding fathers envisioned. In a letter written to James Smith, December 8, 1822 he says:

> *The pure and simple unity of the Creator of the universe, is now all but ascendant in the Eastern States; it is dawning in the West and advancing toward the South; and I confidently expect that the present generation will see Unitarianism become the general religion of the United States.*

The doctrine of the trinity, however, was much too entrenched to be easily dismissed, and those who did not accept the belief were labeled as non-Christian.

The Early Concepts

In Exploring Church History, **Howard Vos** writes:

> *One of the earliest errors was Ebionism. Appearing in fully developed form in the second century, it was in reality only a continuation of the Judaistic opposition to the apostle Paul. Some groups seem to have been quite clear on the essentials of salvation but insisted on law keeping as a way of life. Most appear to have denied the deity of Christ. These views they held in an effort to retain a true monotheism. They put much stress on the law in general and on circumcision and Sabbath keeping in particular. Ebionism practically disappeared by the fifth century. It had little if any lasting effect on the church.*

Who were these Ebionites?

The Encyclopedia Britannica (11th edition) states:

> *Epiphanius with his customary confusion makes two separate sects, Ebionites and Nazarenes. Both names,*

however, refer to <u>*the same people*</u>*, the latter going back to the designation of apostolic times (Acts 24:5)*

> [5] For we have found this man a pestilent fellow, and a mover of sedition among all the Jews throughout the world, and a ringleader of the sect of the Nazarenes.

And the former being the term usually applied to them in the ecclesiastical literature of the 2nd and 3rd centuries. The origin of the Nazarenes or Ebionites as a distinct sect is very obscure, but may be dated with much likelihood from the edict of Hadrian which in 135 finally scattered the old church of Jerusalem.

As mentioned earlier, there was a distinct disagreement between Paul and these believers from Jerusalem who are often referred to in the New Testament as "of the circumcision" or "Judaizers." It is important, however, to note that the dispute was over the application of the law. It was NEVER over the deity of Yeshua. Why? Because Paul's perspective on the subject <u>did not differ</u> from theirs. Most of the dispute over the deity of Yeshua came long after Paul's death.

If these early followers did not believe that Yeshua was God, what did they believe?

In <u>The Orthodox Corruption of Scripture</u>, **Bart Ehrman** writes:

> *According to orthodox sources, the Ebionites self-consciously traced their lineage back to the apostolic times, and like the earliest followers of Jesus worked to preserve their Jewish identity and customs, including the practices of circumcision and kashrut.*
>
> *They are most commonly portrayed as adoptionists who reject both the notion of Jesus' pre-existence and the doctrine of his virgin birth, maintaining instead that Jesus was a "normal" human being, born of natural generation. God chose him to be his Son at his baptism*

and gave him his messianic mission. This he fulfilled by dying on the cross, after which God raised him from the dead and exalted him to heaven.

Sources agree that the Ebionites accepted the binding authority of the Old Testament (and therefore the continuing validity of the Law) but rejected the authority of the apostate apostle, Paul.

The sources do not agree about the character and contours of the gospel used by the Ebionites. Most of the fathers from the early second century (Papias) to the late fourth (Jerome) claim that it comprised a truncated form of Matthew (outwardly the most Jewish of the four) written in Hebrew, one that lacked it's opening chapters, that is, the narrative of Jesus' miraculous birth.

Why was this early Hebrew text different from the Greek? The natural assumption is that the Ebionites simply deleted the text that they disagreed with. However, there is no historic evidence that this group was in the practice of altering or deleting text to conform to their particular beliefs.

The evidence, however, is overwhelming that those who espoused the doctrine concerning the deity of Jesus not only altered and added to the text, they did so frequently and as a matter of course.

This was not generally done to mislead or deceive, but in a sincere effort to "clarify" the text. The result, however, is thousands of verifiably corrupted documents that were used in the compiling of various texts we now call the New Testament.

The Development of "Christology"

Additional "clarification" efforts brought about the formation of various "Christologies" which were a natural progression of attempts to justify the Hebraic scriptures through a Greek philosophy perspective.

In time four Christologies developed.

Funk & Wagnalls New Encyclopedia (volume 6 / Christology)

In the New Testament

> *The earliest Christians expressed their explicit Christology with titles and mythological patterns borrowed from the religious environment of 1st century Palestine, where both Hebraic and Hellenistic Greek conceptions of God, history, and destiny were at work. Especially important in a consideration of New Testament Christology is the pervasive eschatological consciousness of the period; many modern scholars think that Jesus himself shared in this consciousness of living at the end of time.*
>
> *Four early patterns of christological thinking can be discerned within the New Testament. The earliest of these has two focuses – looking backward to Jesus' earthly life as that of an eschatological prophet and servant of God and forward to Christ's coming again as the Messiah, the Son of man.*
>
> *In a second two-stage christological formulation the earthly Jesus was also seen as the prophet-servant of the last days, but at the same time he was declared to have become Lord, Christ, and Son of God at his resurrection and exaltation.*
>
> *In the third pattern, these post resurrection titles were applied retrospectively to Jesus in his earthy period in order to articulate the intrinsic connection between Jesus' earthy ministry and his role as savior. A "sending formula" developed, with God as subject, his Son as object, and a statement of saving purpose, as in John 3:16: "For God so loved the world that he*

gave his only Son, that whoever believes in him should not parish but have eternal life" (also Gal. 4:4).

... In the fourth pattern, expressed in the christological hymns of the Hellenistic-Jewish church, Jesus was identified with the Divine Wisdom, or Logos. Philosophical Hellenistic Judaism had conceived of the Logos as the personified agent of the divine being, the agent of creation, revelation, and redemptive action. The earthy Jesus was now seen as the incarnation of this preexistent wisdom or Logos.

... Consequently, "Son of God" and "Son," which were originally terms expressive of Jesus' role in salvation history, acquire a metaphysical import and come to denote his divine being.

The Son of God

Many of the Hebraic phrases and abstract concepts were foreign to the new Gentile leaders. Much of the confusion over the divinity of Yeshua began with the first century messianic title, "Son of God." The Gentiles understood this phrase to mean, "God the Son." Again, this was not an effort to deceive anyone. It was simply the most natural interpretation for someone in the Greek culture to have.

In The Doctrine of the Trinity **Sir Anthony Buzzard** and **Charles Hunting** write:

Responsible historians, both secular and religious, agree that the Jews of Jesus' time held firmly to a faith in a unipersonal God.

Church history shows that the concept of even two equal persons in the Godhead – the Father and Son – did not receive formal approval in the Christian community until three hundred years after the ministry of Jesus, at the Council of Nicea in 325 AD.

This is not to ignore the controversy that came about as a result of Jesus' claim to be the "Son of God." But that claim should not be confused with the much later assertion by the Church that he was "God, the Son." [pp 29, 6, 37]

The first century was a time of expectation. There were many people who were "looking" for the Messiah.

John 1:40

[40]One of the two, which heard John, and followed him, was Andrew, Simon Peter's brother.
[41]He, first found his own brother Simon, and said to him, We have found the Messiah.
[42]And he brought him to Yeshua. And when Yeshua saw him, he said, You are Simon, the son of Jona: you shall be called Cephas, which means: a stone.
[43]The following day, Yeshua went to Galilee, and found Philip, and said to him, Follow me.
[44]Now Philip was from Bethsaida, the city of Andrew and Peter.
[45]Philip finds Nathanael and says to him, We have found him, of whom Moses in the law, and the prophets wrote. Yeshua of Nazareth, the son of Joseph.
[46]And Nathanael said to him, Can anything good come out of Nazareth? Philip said to him, Come and see.
[47]Yeshua saw Nathanael coming to him, and said, Look an Israelite indeed, in whom is no guile!
[48]Nathanael said to him, How do you know me? Yeshua answered and said to him, Before Philip called you, when you were under the fig tree, I saw you.

> [49]*Nathanael answered, and said to him, Rabbi, you are the Son of God, you are the king of Israel.*

Were John and Nathanael proclaiming that Yeshua was God? No, the title, "Son of God," is a Messianic title. They WERE claiming that they believed that Yeshua was the Messiah, they were NOT saying that he was God.

Let's explore other places where we see references to the son(s) of God. In the book of Exodus we see the children of Israel called God's son.

Exodus 4:22

> [22]*And you shall say to Pharaoh, Thus says the LORD, Israel is my son, my firstborn.*
> [23]*And I say to you, Let my son go, that he may serve me: and if you refuse to let him go, I will slay your son, your firstborn*

The phrase, "son of God," is found 46 times in the Bible (only once in the Tanakh / Old Testament). The phrase "sons of God" (plural) is found 11 times in the Bible (five times in the Tanakh / Old Testament).

The one place in the Old Testament where the phrase, "son of God," is used is in Daniel 3:25. This is often used as a "proof" of Yeshua's pre-existence. Since Yeshua is called the "Son of God" in the New Testament, it is reasoned that this Old Testament reference must refer to him also. Is that what is being talked about here?

Daniel 3:25

> [25]*He answered and said, Lo, I see four men loose, walking in the midst of the fire, and they have no hurt; and the form of the fourth is like the son of God.*

In Jewish tradition this fourth man walking in the fire is an angel of God. The places in the Old Testament where the phrase "sons of God" is found, especially those in the book of Job (1:16, 2:1, and 38:7), are also thought to be a reference to angelic beings. The phrase, however, can also mean followers or chosen of God. Certainly most all of the places you see in the New Testament would be read this way.

John 1:12

> [12]*But as many as receive him, to them he gave power to become the sons of God, to them that believe on his name.*

Romans 8:14

> [14]*For as many as are lead by the spirit of God, they are the sons of God.*

Philippians 2:15

> [15]*That you may be blameless and harmless, the sons of God, without rebuke, in the midst of a crooked and perverse nation, among whom you shine as lights in the world,*

1 John 3:1,2

> [1]*Behold, what manner of love the Father has bestowed on us, that we should be called the sons of God: therefore the world knows us not, because it knew him not.*
> [2]*Beloved, now are we the sons of God, and it does not yet appear what we shall be; but we know that when he shall appear, we shall be like him; for we shall see him as he is.*

Paul tells us (Romans 8:14) that anyone who is led by the spirit is a "son of God"; and John tells us (1 John 3:1-2) that "we" are "now" the "sons of God." Paul and John were certainly not suggesting that WE are God.

Who Am I?

Sometimes it is helpful to look at more than one testimony of the same event to fully see what is being said. When Yeshua asked his talmidim (disciples) who they believed he was, we see that Mark, Luke, and Matthew each have a slightly different version of the event.

Mark 8:29

> [29]*And he said to them, But whom do you say I am? And Peter answered and said to him, You are the* <u>*Messiah*</u>*.*

Luke 9:20

> [20]*And he said to them, But whom do you say I am? Peter answering said, The* <u>*Messiah*</u> *(or the anointed)* <u>*of God*</u>*.*

Matthew 16:15-16

> [15]*He said to them, But Whom do you say I am?* [16]*And Simon Peter answered and said, You are the* <u>*Messiah*</u>*, the* <u>*son of the living God.*</u>

Here Peter is proclaiming that he believes Yeshua is the Messiah; he is <u>not</u> saying that he is God.

The Return of the Exiles

Where else in scripture do we find the phrase, "son(s) of the living God"? It is found in the first chapter of the book of Hosea. Hosea was a prophet to Israel (the northern kingdom) during the time of the divided kingdom.

Hosea 1:10-11

> [10]*Yet the number of the children of Israel shall be as the sand of the sea, which cannot be measured or numbered; and it shall come to pass, in the place where it was said to them,*

> *You are not my people, there it shall be said to them, you are the sons of the living God.* [11]*Then shall the children of Judah and the children of Israel be gathered together, and appoint themselves one head, and they shall come up out of the land; for great shall be the day of Jezreel.*

In this passage we see the northern kingdom (the House of Israel), who lost their identity because they would not follow God's instructions, brought back from exile at the end of the age, and will be reunited with the southern kingdom (Judah).

The redemption of the northern kingdom of Israel is a pivotal point in future prophetic events. After this happens is when the messianic age is ushered in. Paul refers to this Romans 8.

Romans 8:19

> [19]*For the earnest expectation of the creation waits for the manifestation of the sons of God.*

But what does THAT have to do with Jesus (Yeshua)?

Chapter 10
Who Did Jesus Think He Was?

It may surprise you to find out that Jesus (Yeshua) did NOT believe that he was THE Messiah. He did, however believe that he was A messiah (one who was anointed [chosen]).

In **Matthew 10:34** Yeshua says:

> *Think not that I am come to send peace on earth: I came not to send peace, but a sword.*

This passage is somewhat problematic. After all THE Messiah's main purpose is to bring peace to the earth. So what exactly is Yeshua talking about?

The Two Messiahs

A belief in Orthodox Judaism is that two Messiahs will usher in the end of the age; Messiah son of Joseph (the suffering servant), and Messiah son of David (the conquering king).

According to tradition, Messiah ben-Joseph will enable events to bring the two kingdoms (Judah and Israel) back together. However, through this effort Messiah ben-Joseph will die. His death also brings a time of war and destruction.

After this happens, Messiah ben-David will rule both houses of Israel with the Third Temple built in Jerusalem as the center of worship, and an era of peace comes for the entire world.

Messiah ben Joseph

From the **Talmud** (Sukkot 52a) we read:

> *What is the cause of mourning [referring to Zechariah 12:10]? R. Dosa and the Rabbis differ on the point. One explained, The cause is the slaying of Messiah*

> *the son of Joseph, and the other explained, The cause is the slaying of the Evil Inclination.*
>
> *It is well, according to him who explains, that the cause is the slaying of Messiah the son of Joseph, since that well agrees with Scriptual verse, "And they shall look upon me because they have thrust him through, and they shall mourn for him as one mourns for his only son."*

Again, from Sukkot 52a we read [as an interpretation of Psalm 2:7]:

> *Our Rabbis taught, The Holy One, blessed be He, will say to the Messiah, son of David (may he reveal himself speedily in our days!), "Ask of me anything, and I will give it to you," as it is said, "I will tell of the decree etc. this day have I begotten you, ask of me and I will give the nations for your inheritance." But when he will see that the Messiah the son of Joseph is slain, he will say to Him, "Lord of the Universe, I ask of You only the gift of life." "As to life," He would answer him, "Your father David has already prophesied this concerning you," as it is said, He asked life of you, you gave it to him, [even length of days for ever and ever].*

Messiah is God's agent through whom Israel realizes its redemption. But, remember, there are two Messiahs in Jewish theology; Messiah ben Joseph, then Messiah ben David. It is the death of Messiah ben Joseph that brings the two kingdoms of Israel together.

So it is Messiah ben Joseph who "saves" the northern kingdom.

What did Yeshua say about who he was to save?

Luke 19:10

> *For the Son of man is come to seek and to save that which was lost.*

Things Lost

Yeshua also talks quite often about things that are lost, comparing those things to the kingdom of God. Luke records a number of stories in the 15th chapter.

Luke 15:4

> [4]*What man of you, having an hundred sheep, if he lose one of them, does not leave the ninety and nine in the wilderness, and go after that which is lost, until he finds it?*

Luke 15:8

> [8]*Or what woman having ten pieces of silver, if she loses one piece, does not light a candle and sweep the house, and seek diligently till she finds it?*

Luke 15:32

> [32]*It was fitting that we should make merry, and be glad: for this your brother was dead, and is alive again; and was lost, and is found.*

Who specifically did Yeshua say he was sent to?

Matthew 15:24

> [24]*I am not sent but to the lost sheep of the house of Israel.*

Who did Yeshua send his 12 disciples to?

Matthew 10:5

> [5]*Yeshua instructed these twelve as he sent them out: "Do not go into the territory of the gentiles; and do not go into any city of the Samaritans.*
> [6]*Go, rather, to the lost sheep of the House of Israel.*
> [7]*As you go, proclaim: The kingdom of Heaven is near.*

In the first century there was no doubt about who he was referring to. The northern kingdom is often referred to as the "Lost" Ten Tribes. Also, in prophecy the "House of Israel" and the "House of Judah" are the northern and southern kingdoms. He is not ambiguous. By saying that he only came for the "the lost sheep of the House of Israel" means that he did not come for the Jews and he did not come for the Gentiles.

A great rabbi known as **Malbim** from the 1800's writes:

> *A transformation will take place. The Ten Tribes and the stick of Joseph will draw themselves closer unto the stick of Judah, and this too, will be through the agency of a Prophet and by miracles.*

In the first century, as people in the society around them began to speculate on the miracles that he performed, many people believed that Yeshua was the Messiah.

John 7:31-35

> [31]*And many of the people believed on him, and said, "When Messiah comes, will he do more miracles than these which this [man] has done?"*

> [32]*The Pharisees heard that the people murmured such things concerning him; and the Pharisees and the chief priests sent officers to take him.*
> [33]*Then Yeshua said to them, "Yet a little while am I with you, and then I go to him that sent me.*
> [34]*You shall seek me, and shall not find [me]: and where I am, there you cannot come."*
> [35]*Then said the Judeans among themselves, where will he go that we shall not find him? Will he go to the dispersed among the Gentiles?"*

Why did they respond by saying, "Will he go to the dispersed among the Gentiles?" They responded this way because they knew that is what Messiah was to do; go to those who were dispersed – the lost ten tribes.

This, however, was a confusing thing, even to his disciples. They knew that Messiah was to bring about the return of the northern kingdom, and yet Yeshua didn't seem to accomplish this task. Even during their last contact, the restoration of Israel was what they were waiting for and expecting to happen.

Acts 1:6

> [6]*When they therefore were come together, they asked of him, saying, Lord, will you at this time restore again the kingdom to Israel?*
> [7]*And he said to them, It is not for you to know the times or the seasons, which the Father has put in his own power.*

Israel went into captivity hundreds of years before this time. But they were to be restored at the end of the age.

In Every Man's Talmud **Abraham Cohen** writes:

> *Another confirmed belief was that the Messiah would affect the reunion of the tribes of Israel. While we find the teaching, 'The ten tribes will have no share in the World to Come' (Tosifta Sanh,XIII.12), the Talmud usually takes the opposite view. By appealing to such text as Is.xxvii.13 and Jer.iii.12, the Rabbis enunciated the doctrine of the return of the lost ten tribes (Sanh.110b). 'Great will be the day when the exiles of Israel will be reassembled as the day when heaven and earth were created'(Pes.88a).*

The early followers of Yeshua believed that Isaiah prophesied about Yeshua in passages like Isaiah 53:5. Today, these passages are often interpreted as referring to Israel as a nation, however, **Martin Jaffee** points out:

> *The identity of this divine servant is given as Israel, but the servant is also to "raise up the tribes of Jacob." Is Israel, then, its own redeemer?*

Since Messiah ben Joseph comes first, what should we look for and how do we know when he will come?

We know that Messiah ben David will be a descendant of King David, but what about Messiah ben Joseph? Will he be a descendant of Joseph?

Maybe. That is certainly one possibility. However, one reason given for him to have this title is because he, at first, is not known. Just as Joseph reveals himself to his brothers, so too will the identity of Messiah ben Joseph remain hidden, until he is revealed.

The 9th chapter of the book of Daniel is often called the "Seventy Weeks Prophecy" (490 years). Many people of the first century believed this prophecy predicted when the Messiah would come.

Daniel lived in Judea 100 years after the northern kingdom (Israel) had been taken into captivity by the Assyrians. When Daniel was a young man, Jerusalem and the first Temple were destroyed and the nation of Judah was also taken captive. Daniel grew up in Babylon where he wrote this prophecy.

Daniel 9:26

> [26]*But after 62 weeks (434 years) the Messiah will be killed but not for himself; then the people of the prince shall come and destroy the city (Jerusalem) and the sanctuary (Temple); and the end thereof shall be with a flood and unto the end of the war desolations are determined.*

There are two points to consider when reading this prophecy. First, if Daniel wrote this prophecy after the first Temple had ALREADY been destroyed, then this prophecy is about the destruction of the SECOND Temple. Daniel received this prophecy BEFORE the second Temple had EVEN been built.

Second, this is NOT a prophecy about Messiah ben David, because THIS Messiah is killed. It is a prophecy about Messiah ben Joseph.

NOTICE that Messiah comes and THEN the Temple is destroyed. The second Temple was destroyed in 70 CE (AD). It is Messiah ben Joseph's death that brings the exiles back, allowing the northern and southern kingdom to once again be brought together. How can this be, since the exiles of the northern kingdom (an event saved until the end of the age) have not yet returned?

What exactly does the prophecy say?

It says that Messiah ben Joseph dies before the second Temple is destroyed. It does not say anything about the return of the exiles. However, we know from other sources that it is BECAUSE of his death the exiles return, but the return does not happen UNTIL the end of the age.

Could Yeshua, then, be Messiah ben Joseph? Clearly this is who he believed he was. There have also been others that seem to have speculated this. In the New Testament there is a story about Caiaphas, the high priest.

John 11:47-53

> [47]*Then gathered the chief priests and the Pharisees a council, and said, "What can we do? for this man does many miracles.*
> [48]*If we let him alone, all [men] will believe on him: and the Romans shall come and take away both our place and nation."*
> [49]*And one of them, [named] Caiaphas, being the high priest that same year, said to them, "You know nothing at all,*
> [50]*nor consider that it is expedient for us, that one man should die for the people, and that the whole nation perish not."*
> [51]*And he spoke not of himself: but being high priest that year, he prophesied that Yeshua should die for that nation;*
> [52]*And not for that nation only, but that he also should gather together in one the children of God that were scattered abroad.*
> [53]*Then from that day on they plotted to put him to death.*

Why would they plot to kill someone whom they believed was Messiah?

It is difficult to know how much alteration to the text has happened in order to "clarify", but IF Caiaphas believed that Yeshua was Messiah Ben Joseph he also believed that Yeshua MUST DIE in order for the northern kingdom to return, and ALL of Israel be united as one under the rulership of Messiah Ben David.

Yeshua refers to this "death plot" (quoting from Psalm 35:19) a few chapters later in **John 15:25**

> [25]*But this happened that the word might be fulfilled which is written in the law, "They hated me without a cause."*

If, indeed, Yeshua (and others) believed that he was Messiah ben Joseph, his death would have had a tremendous impact on those around him. There would be an anticipation of the end time. And although the next few years seemed to be a time of relative peace, looking at the larger picture, this was NOT a time of peace at all.

A Time of Anguishing Events

The first century is known for some very devastating historic events. Christianity looks to the life and death of Yeshua, and in Judaism one of the most anguishing events was the destruction of the second Temple.

In Tractate Yoma of the **Talmud** it says:

> *Why was the first Holy Temple destroyed? Because of three wicked things: idol worship, adultery, and murder. But in the second Temple in which time the Jewish people were occupied studying the Torah and doing good deeds and acts of charity why was it then destroyed?*
>
> *The answer is: It was because of hatred without a cause to teach you, that hate without a cause is equal to these sins and that it is as serious a crime as the three great transgressions of idol worship, adultery, and murder. [Yoma 9]*

Remember, years earlier Yeshua had given this as the very reason he would be killed (hatred without a cause). Also throughout the New Testament he compares his death to the destruction of the Temple.

John 2:19

> [19]*Yeshua answered and said to them, Destroy this temple, and in three days I will raise it up.*
> [20]*Then said the Jews, Forty and six years was this temple in building, and will you rear it up in three days?*
> [21]*But he spoke of the temple of his body.*

So, what was the controversy leading to his death? No one knows exactly why a Rabbi from Galilee with about 150 followers caused so much concern for the nation's leaders in Jerusalem. However, it seems to be not just religiously, but also politically motivated.

In addition, the controversies that existed during his life did not diminish with his death. Although Yeshua was actually put to death by the Gentiles (Romans), it was his own people (the Sanhedrin) who sentenced him.

According to the **Talmud** the charges against him were that he:

> *performed magic, enticed, and led astray Israel.*

His was sentenced to be stoned to death, then hung for a short time on a wooden cross (or to be more exact a wooden "T").

The Sanhedrin sentencing someone to death, however, was in itself an extremely unusual occurrence.

The **Talmud** says in Tractate Makkot:

> *A Sanhedrin that effects an execution once in seven years is branded a destructive tribunal. Rabbi Eliezer ben Azariah says: Once in seventy years. Rabbi Tarfon and Rabbi Akiva say: Were we members of a Sanhedrin, no person would ever be put to death. [Thereupon] Rabban Simeon ben Gamaliel remarked, [yea] and*

> *they would also multiply shedders of blood in Israel! [Makkot 7a]*

All executions were, by Roman law, to be carried out by the empire.

Whether it was the extreme brutality of the Romans or some disagreement between members of the court, something happened in 30CE that affected the Sanhedrin (the supreme court of first century Judaism) so much they physically removed themselves from the Temple so they could never again impose the death sentence. And indeed the death sentence was never again imposed.

Again, from the **Talmud** in <u>Tractate Avodah Zara</u> it says:

> *Forty years before the Temple was destroyed did the Sanhedrin abandon [the Temple] and held its sittings in Hanuth. Has this any legal bearing?... <u>Capital cases ceased</u>. Why? -- Because when the Sanhedrin saw that murderers were so prevalent that they could not be properly dealt with judicially, they said: Rather let us be exiled from place to place than pronounce them guilty [of capital offences] for it is written: And you shall do according to the sentence, which they of that place which the Lord shall choose shall tell you, which implies that it is the place that matters. [Avodah Zara 8b]*

That, however, was not the only change in the Temple at that time.

Again from Tractate Yoma in the Talmud it says:

> *<u>Forty years before the Holy Temple was destroyed</u> the following things happened: <u>The lot for the Yom Kippur goat</u> ceased to be supernatural; the red cord of wool that used to change to white (as a symbol of God's forgiveness) now remained red and did not change and <u>the western candle</u> in the candlestick in*

the sanctuary refused to burn continually while the doors of the Holy Temple would open of themselves. [Tractate Yoma 39:b]

The Temple was destroyed in 70CE. What a tremendous coincidence in that these things began to happen forty years before the Temple was destroyed; in 30CE, the very year that Yeshua was put to death and died on Nisan 14 on a hill outside the city walls of Jerusalem.

The **Babylonian Talmud** says:

> *Since nothing was brought forward in his favor he was hanged on the eve of Passover. (Sanhedrin 43a)*

So we see that Yeshua himself believed that he was Messiah ben Joseph. But didn't he ALSO believe that he would have a "second coming" as Messiah ben David?

One interesting point to observe is that rarely, if ever, does Yeshua use a first person reference when talking about the end time. He put his statements in the third person, saying "the son of man" will do this or that. We simply assume that "the son of man" is used as a reference to himself.

But if we analyze the text we see that sometimes that assumption does not fit. Lets look again at **Matthew 16:13**

> *When Yeshua came into the coasts of Caesarea Philippi, he asked his disciples, saying, Whom do men say that I the son of man am?*

Although the Greek word "me" (translated as "I") is used here, it is a bit awkward. Why not just say "Who do people say that I am"? Why add the phrase "the son of man"? In it's original form, the text most likely simply asked, "Who do people say that the son of man is?

Again, it was assumed that he was talking about himself, and the word "I" was added for "clarification".

However, with that assumption the answer to the question does not seem to make a lot of sense.

> *And they said, Some [say that you are] John the Baptist. Some, Elijah; and others Jeremiah, or one of the prophets.*

Why would people believe that Yeshua was his cousin, John the Baptist? They knew who John the Baptist was. Were they just confused as to who was who? Did they believe there were two Johns?

Or, why would people believe that Yeshua was Elijah, Jeremiah, or another one of the prophets? Would there be ANY reason for them to believe such a thing?

However, if you understand that the "son of man" and "son of God" are titles, then the answer makes perfect sense.

> *Who do people say the "son of man" (this prophetic person) is?*

They were not claiming that Yeshua was a reincarnation of Jeremiah, rather that Jeremiah may have been this figure known as "the son of man". As I stated earlier, in nearly all end-time descriptions of a Messiah figure, Yeshua uses the third person "son of man". Why is this? Could he have believed that an end-time Messiah might not be him?

In fact he did. We can not only see this from his use of the term "son of man", but he also makes references of "another" one coming.

John 14:16

> *And I will pray the Father, and he shall send you another advocate (messiah), that he may be with you forever.*

John 16:7

> *I tell you the truth; It is expedient for you that I go away: for if I go not away, the advocate*

(messiah) will not come to you.

What does this mean? The Greek church fathers (who later tried to explain and "clarify" what Yeshua had said), were not Torah scholars and certainly knew nothing of the oral traditions. They saw things from their own perspective. They believed in many gods, and it was natural to assume that a messiah was a god.

Unfortunately, not understanding the teaching about Messiah ben Joseph (the messiah that dies) and Messiah ben David (the messiah that "shall teach you all things") lead to a belief that this "other" advocate was the "Holy Spirit" bringing with it (as time went on) the Christian doctrine of the trinity.

The idea that messiah was God, however was NOT part of the doctrines taught by Yeshua and his disciples. That is a controversy that developed much later. To believe that Messiah was God would be a gross misunderstanding of first century concepts and terminology.

So what happened? After all, Messiah ben Joseph's specific purpose and mission is to save Israel (the children of God that were scattered abroad), a task that up to this point remains unfulfilled.

As **Martin Jaffee** writes:

> *Early Jewish followers of Jesus of Nazareth, of course, had seen in him the fulfillment of Messianic promises. But he had died a criminal's death and left the world in Exile entirely as it had been, tales of his resurrection notwithstanding.*

However, **Rabbi Pinchas Winston** writes:

> *Moshiach Ben Yosef's success, by our standard of measurement, is a limited one. Not only will he be, or perhaps already is (or even already was), human, he will be humanly vulnerable. In fact, according to one*

> *opinion in the Talmud, Moshiach Ben Yosef will leave this world without being able to see the fruits of his labors.*

What does THAT mean? It is strange to think that both "branches" of "Christianity" failed at accomplishing their mission. The Gentiles, who were suppose to be Noahide supporters of the Jews, instead became persecutors, and Yeshua (who believed he was Messiah ben Joseph) along with the Jewish leaders, never did find the Lost Tribes that were exiled. Most of them, within a short time, died violent deaths at the hands of pagans.

Judging Christianity from its first hundred years, it was a miserable failure. So what was it all for? Why did Christianity even come into existence?

Chapter 11
Why Christianity?

What a dilemma we have as we look at the origins of Christianity, and compare it to the modern church. The original goals and intentions of Christianity were never realized and yet, as a religion, it has grown into something that has definitely changed the world.

What has caused this to happen? If God has planned everything from the beginning, what is the reason for Christianity? Was God creating a new religion? If so, why? If not, what is He doing?

It is evident, from reading the Bible, that the plan of God involves his chosen people, Israel. And yet, if the end time prophecies of the Bible focus on the Jewish population, how do Christians fit in?

Just by looking at the world around us, you would have to conclude that Christianity is ALSO part of God's plan. In fact, it seems to be an essential part; without it the world would be a much different place.

How has Christianity affected the world? Let's stop for a moment and consider the impact that the Christian faith has had. It has been the Christian religion that has brought the Holy Scriptures (the Tanakh or Old Testament) to the world. If it were not for Christianity publishing and distributing Bibles to the most remote parts of the world, the knowledge of the God of Abraham, Isaac, and Jacob would be limited to whatever Jewish communities there happened to be; and western civilization, which is for the most part a Bible based society would only exist within those Jewish communities.

The concepts of messiah and a future redemption, along with sayings like, "Love your neighbor as yourself" and "Do unto others as you would have them do unto you", although Jewish in origin, have been presented to the greater population through the Christian faith.

In addition, much of the humanitarian efforts in the world today are sponsored by Christian organizations.

Christianity seems to have affected the world in dramatic ways, and yet when you read through the the prophecies of the Bible about the end times, there is little (if any) indication of its existence.

There have been several attempts to solve the apparent gap in the Bible when it comes to recognizing the Christian faith outside of the New Testament.

Three Christian Theologies

Three prominent theological perspectives that attempt to bridge that gap are: Replacement Theology, Dispensational Theology, and Covenant Theology.

Replacement Theology is basically where the word "Christianity" simply replaces the word "Israel" wherever it is mentioned (in a positive way) in end-time Bible prophecy.

Dispensationalists believe that God works with different people at different times in different ways. God's laws, therefore, are not universal but, rather, are the somewhat arbitrary guidelines he uses at different times throughout history.

Covenant Theology is where God's relationship with people is dependent upon the covenant or agreements between them.

All of these views have the same basic premise. The Jews WERE God's chosen people who were given certain laws UNTIL he sent their messiah to them. Since they rejected their messiah, God rejected them and chose a NEW people and new set of laws.

The problem is that the Bible simply does not support this premise.

What then is going on? Does God still consider the Jews his chosen people, or has he chosen a new group of people? How does this strange relationship between Jew and Christian fit into God's plan? Do Jews need to convert to Christianity in order to be saved or must all Christians become Jewish?

Again, what is Christianity all about? Was Christianity all just a big mistake? Why was so much misunderstood? Why didn't it's founders seem to accomplish their mission? ...Why Christianity?

Maimonides, a rabbi from the 13th century, hinted at Christianity being a transitional religion. Transitioning from what, or to what?

The New Covenant

God has a chosen people. He has NOT chosen ANOTHER people. EVEN when He makes a new covenant, He does so with the House of Israel and the House of Judah. He does not makes a covenant with Gentiles.

Jeremiah 31:31-34 & Hebrews 8:8-12

> [31]*Look! The days are coming, says the LORD, when I will make a new covenant with the House of Israel, and with the House of Judah:*
> [32]*Not according to the covenant that I made with their fathers in the day that I took them by the hand to bring them out of the land of Egypt. They broke my covenant even though I was a husband to them, says the LORD.*
> [33]*But this is the covenant that I will make with the House of Israel at that time, says the LORD, I will put my Torah into their very being, and write it in their hearts; and will be their God, and they will be my people.*

Again, NOTICE the NEW covenant is NOT made with Gentiles. It is made with the WHOLE nation of Israel (both houses), where God will write His laws on the hearts of the House of ISRAEL. Why doesn't he write His laws on the hearts of the House of Judah?

Hosea 1:6b-7

> *I will no more have mercy upon the house of Israel; but I will utterly take them away. But I will have mercy upon the house of Judah, and will save them by the LORD their God, and will not save them by bow, nor by sword, nor by battle, by horses, nor by horsemen.*

Saving the Jews

In November of 2001 the Vatican issued a 210 page report entitled The Jewish People and the Holy Scriptures in the Christian Bible. In this document, the top theologians of the Roman Catholic Church have made some significant paradigm shifts.

According to **Eugene Fisher** of the National Conference of Catholic Bishops:

> *"We don't need to work or pray for the conversion of Jews to Christianity. God already has the salvation of the Jews figured out, and they accepted it on Sinai, so they are OK. Jews are already with the Father. We do not have a mission to the Jews, but only a mission with the Jews to the world. The Catholic Church will never again sanction an organization devoted to the conversion of Jews. That is over, on doctrinal, biblical and pastoral grounds."*

The Catholic Church is citing "biblical" grounds for this new teaching which has become official church doctrine. So, what do the Scriptures say about the Jews and salvation? In **John 4:22** Yeshua says:

> *You worship what you do not know; we know what we worship, for salvation is of the Jews.*

Many people make the mistake of believing that Yeshua thought his mission was to save the Jews. Clearly this is not the case. Neither did he believe his mission was to "graft in" Gentiles.

The mission of Meshiah ben Joseph (who Yeshua believed he was) is to save the Lost Sheep of the House of Israel. It is the House of ISRAEL who needs to return to God, not Judah.

Messiah ben Joseph is to redeem and to die for ISRAEL's sins; NOT the House of Judah and NOT the Gentiles.

In **Acts 5:31** is reads:

> *God exalted with his right hand [to be] a prince and a saviour, for to give repentance to ISRAEL and forgivness of sins.*

So what does this have to do with Christianity? Remember what Maimonides said. Christianity is a transitional religion. Christianity transitioned the the world from Greek polytheism to the belief in the God of Abraham Isaac and Jacob. It has spread throughout the entire world, and yet developed and retained enough paganism to be unacceptable as a branch of Judaism.

Although Christianity developed quite differently from what it's founders had intended, it would appear that this is certainly part of a master plan for humanity.

Christianity, however, is not a replacement of Judaism. Rather, Christianity could be viewed as a VEHICLE by which God will bring back the LOST <u>House of Israel</u> from exile, reuniting them with the House of Judah.

Hosea 1:11

> [11]*Then shall the children of Judah and the children of Israel be gathered together, and appoint themselves one head, and they shall come up out of the land: for great shall be the day of Jezreel.*

All end time prophecy is fixed around one major event; the return of the Lost Ten Tribes of Israel. Even though God had exiled Israel, and removed its identity, God promised to gather them again.

Jeremiah 29:14

> *You will find me, says the LORD, and I will reverse your exile. I will gather you from all the nations, and from all the places to which I have banished you, says the LORD. I will bring you back to the place from which I exiled you.*

The prophet Hosea tells what the history of the house of Israel (the Ten Tribes) will be in the first chapter of his book.

Hosea 1:2

> [2]*...And the LORD said to Hosea, Go, take unto thee a wife of whoredoms and children of whoredoms: for the land hath committed great whoredom, departing from the LORD.*
> [3]*So he went and took Gomer the daughter of Diblaim; which conceived, and bare him a son.*
> [4]*And the LORD said unto him, Call his name Jezreel; for* yet a little while*, and I will avenge the blood of Jezreel upon the house of Jehu, and will cause to cease the kingdom of the house of Israel.*
> [5]*And it shall come to pass at that day, that I will break the bow of Israel in the valley of Jezreel.*

[6]*And she conceived again, and bore a daughter. And God said to him, Call her name Loru-ha-mah: for I will have* <u>*no mercy*</u> *anymore upon the house of Israel; but I will utterly take them away.*
[7]*But I will have mercy on the house of Judah, and will save them by the LORD their God, and will not save them by bow, nor by sword, nor by battle, by horses, nor by horsemen.*
[8]*Now when she had weaned Loru-ha-mah, she conceived, and bore a son.*
[9]*Then said God, Call his name Lo-ammi: for you are* <u>*not my people*</u>*, and I will not be your God.*
[10]*Yet the number of the children of Israel shall be as the sand of the sea, which cannot be measured nor numbered; and it shall come to pass, that in the place where it was said to them, You are not my people, there it shall be said to them, You are the* <u>*sons of the living God*</u>*.*

"Son of the living God" is a Messianic title that refers back to this passage in Hosea, because it is through the efforts of Messiah ben Joseph that the House of Israel will return. Remember how the apostle Peter refers back to this passage. When Yeshua asks his disciples who they believed he was, Peter answered:

Matthew 16:16

[16]*And Simon Peter answered and said, You are the Messiah,* <u>*the son of the living God*</u>*.*

Again, Peter was not saying that Yeshua was God, rather he was saying that Yeshua was the messiah who helps bring about the return of the lost tribes.

Later Peter, in his own writings, would allude to Hosea to indicate that the purpose of Christianity was to reach the lost sheep of the House of Israel (Hosea 1:6-10):

1 Peter 2:10

> [10] *Which in time past were not a people, but are now the people of God: which had not obtained mercy, but now have obtained mercy.*

Fishers of Men

At the beginning of his ministry Yeshua tells his talmidim that they will be "fishers of men."

Matthew 4:19

> [19] *And he said to them, Follow me, and I will make you fishers of men.*

The reference to "fishers" is also found in the writings of the prophet Jeremiah. This again is in reference to the House of Israel returning to both the land and to God.

Jeremiah 1:11

> [16] *Behold, I will send for many fishers, says the LORD, and they shall fish them; and after will I send for many hunters, and they shall hunt them from every mountain, and from every hill, and out of the holes of the rocks.*

This passage seems to put the redemption of Israel in two stages, using first fishers, and then hunters.

According to the prophets, the redemption of the House of Israel (the Lost Ten Tribes) does not happen till the end of the age. How then does God accomplish this task?

God is not arbitrary. His laws are consistent, and He doesn't make mistakes. God has not changed or done away with his laws. The word of God and His commandments are the same as they have always been.

1John 2:7

> [7]*Brethren, I write no new commandment unto you, but an old commandment which ye had from the beginning. The old commandment is the word which ye have heard from the beginning.*

The End From the Beginning

God also has had His plan for mankind from the beginning. God knows exactly where He is going.

Isaiah 46:9

> [9]*Remember the former things, those of long ago; I am God, and there is no other; I am God, and there is none like me.*
> [10]*I make known the end from the beginning, from ancient times, what is still to come. I say: My purpose will stand, and I will do all that I please.*

As the Israelites were in the desert in the wilderness, God told them about their return from exile.

Deuteronomy 30:1

> [2]*and when you and your children return to the LORD your God and obey him with all your heart and with all your soul according to everything I command you today,*
> [3]*then the LORD your God will restore your fortunes and have compassion on you and gather you again from all the nations where he scattered you.*
> [4]*Even if you have been banished to the most distant land under the heavens, from there the LORD your God will gather you and bring you back.*

John 10:16

> [16]*And other sheep I have, which are not of this fold: them also I must bring, and they shall hear my voice; and there shall be one fold, [and] one shepherd.*

So if the plan of God was to redeem Israel, why didn't he do it in the first century? Because he would NOT redeem Israel until the END of the age.

This may explain Yeshua's strange explanation as to why he spoke in parables.

Matthew 13:10

> [10]*And the disciples came, and asked him, Why do you speak to them in parables?*
> [11]*He answered and said, Because it is given to you to know the mysteries of the kingdom of heaven, but to them it is not given.*
> *...*[14]*And in them is fulfilled the prophecy of Isaiah, which says, "By hearing you shall hear, and shall not understand; and seeing you shall see, and shall not perceive:*
> [15]*For this people's heart is waxed gross, and [their] ears are dull of hearing, and their eyes they have closed; lest at any time they should see with [their] eyes, and hear with [their] ears, and should understand with [their] heart, and should be converted, and I should heal them."*

Who is God talking to Isaiah about? And why wouldn't God want to heal these people? This is the nation of Israel that God would punish by taking away the knowledge of who they were till the end of the age. The first century simply was NOT THE TIME for the Lost Tribes to remember and return, but it was necessary to set up a mechanism for the return when that time arrived.

So, who are the Lost Ten Tribes of Israel and when will they return?

Chapter 12
WHO is the House of Israel?

A Rabbi of Rabbis

We walked to a small park in an ultra orthodox neighborhood of Jerusalem in the fall of 2002. Then sitting down on a couple of park benches we began to talk. The Rabbi that we were talking to was introduced to us as a Rabbi of Rabbis. The meeting had been arranged for us to discuss the movement within Christianity in which Christians are being drawn to a more Jewish way of life. I began by posing the question, "If there are Christians being drawn to their Hebrew roots ..." The Rabbi stopped me. "Let's not say 'if'," he said, "We know its happening". For a moment I was struck speechless. I began again. "Could this phenomenon that is going on … be the northern kingdom (House of Israel) returning?", I asked. The Rabbi cocked his head to the side, "Maybe yes, maybe no. We will have to wait and see."

No Magic Wand

So who exactly is the House of Israel? Rabbi Chaim Richman from the Temple Institute in Jerusalem says "There is no magic wand" for detecting who or where the House of Israel is. The Lost Tribes have vanished from history. They are, after all, LOST! Although many people have traced genealogies, looked at languages and cultural practices, and studied archeology, the question of who and where the Lost Ten Tribes are, is still one of the greatest mysteries of history.

I propose that we don't need to know WHO or WHERE they are ... only that they ARE. They will become self evident.

One tradition in Judaism is that the lost souls of Israel will be redeemed as a "spark of holiness".

Holy Sparks

The **Lubavitcher Rebbe** teaches:

> *The Talmud offers the following explanation for the* ***phenomenon of galut****: "The people of Israel were exiled amongst the nations only so that converts might be added to them."*
>
> ***On the most basic level****, this is a reference to the many* ***non-Jews who****, in the course of the centuries of our dispersion, have come in contact with the Jewish people and have been inspired to* ***convert to Judaism****.*
>
> *But Chassidic teaching explains that the Talmud is also referring to* ***souls*** *of a different sort that are* ***transformed and elevated in the course of our exiles*** *... It is to this end that we have been dispersed across the face of earth: so that we may come in contact with the* ***sparks of holiness that await redemption*** *in every corner of the globe.*

So how does the northern kingdom find it's way back? We know that the Lost Tribes have assimilated into the nations that they were exiled to. They have become, for all practical purposes, Gentiles. When they return, however, what halacha do they follow? Will it be a standard conversion process where each individual is absorbed into what ever tradition of Judaism they are sponsored into? Some Sephardic, some Ashkenazi, some Chassidic, etc.

The prophets don't indicate that will be the case. In Ezekiel after the vision of the valley of "dry bones" it says:

Ezekiel 37:16

> *... Now Son of Man, take for yourself one piece of wood and write upon it, For Judah and for the Children of Israel, his comrades; and take one piece of wood and write upon it, For Joseph, the wood of Ephraim and all the*

> *House of Israel, his comrades. Then bring them close to yourself, one to the other, like one piece of wood, and they will become united in your hand.*

It appears that for the two nations to become one, there needs to be a recognized northern kingdom. As that northern kingdom moves from being Gentile to once again part of God's chosen people, they will travel on a path where they may be expected to adhere to a certain halacha. The first and most obvious stage of observance is that of the Noachide. This was how Israel first began their observances from Sinai.

Rabbi Elijah Benamozegh, in his book "Israel and Humanity" [p.245], writes:

> *When Mosaism is born, Noachism forms the first step of the ladder which the Israelite must climb before attaining the Mosaic Law. Thus, when Israel went out of Egypt, it was first of all introduced to the Noachide Law, and only after this preliminary initiation did it receive the law of Moses. "Moses went out and repeated to the people all the commands [divrei] of the Lord and all the rules [mishpatim]." (Exodus 24:3) Of this verse, the sages say:*
>
> > *The commands of the Lord are the ordinances relating to the proper behavior which the people had to observe while waiting at the foot of Sinai; the rules are the seven precepts of the sons of Noah. [Rashi]*

When the northern kingdom becomes evident, their observances will begin to change and develop.

No one can say exactly how the House of Israel will return from exile, (and, for all practical purposes, non-existence). However, all of the prophets agree that at the end of the age they WILL return.

Malachi 3:7 & 4:1-6

> [7]*Even from the days of your fathers you have gone away from my ordinances, and have not kept them. Return to me, and I will return to you, says the LORD of hosts. But you said, Wherein shall we return?*

The House of Israel will at first, however, not believe that they NEED to return.

> [13]*Your words have been stout against me, says the LORD. Yet you say, What have we spoken [so much] against you?*
> [14]*You have said, It [is] in vain to serve God; and what profit [is it] that we have kept his ordinances, and that we have walked mournfully before the LORD of hosts?*

They feel that the law has been "done away" with.

> [15]*And now we call the proud happy, yes, they that work wickedness are set up; yes, [they that] tempt God are even delivered.*
> [16]*Then they that feared the LORD spoke often one to another; and the LORD hearkened, and heard [it], and a book of remembrance was written before him for them that feared the LORD, and that thought upon his name.*
> [17]*And they shall be mine, says the LORD of hosts, in that day when I make up my jewels, and I will spare them, as a man spares his own son that serves him.*
> [18]*Then shall you return, and discern between the righteous and the wicked, between him that serves God and him that serves him not.*

It is God's plan that the House of Israel is to RETURN (repent) and remember.

> [4:1] *For, behold, the day comes, that shall burn as an oven, and all the proud, yes, and all that do wickedly, shall be stubble; and the day that comes shall burn them up, says the LORD of hosts that it shall leave them neither root nor branch.*
> [2] *But to you that fear my name shall the Sun of righteousness arise with healing in his wings; and you shall go forth, and grow up as calves of the stall.*
> [3] *And you shall tread down the wicked; for they shall be ashes under the souls of your feet in the day that I shall do [this], says the LORD of hosts.*
> [4] *Remember you the law of Moses my servant, which I commanded to him in Horeb for all Israel, [with] the statutes and judgments.*
> [5] *Behold, I will send you Elijah the prophet before the coming of the great and dreadful day of the LORD;*
> [6] *And he shall turn the heart of the fathers to the children, and the heart of the children to their fathers, lest I come and smite the earth with a curse.*

Elijah, the great prophet to the northern kingdom (the House of Israel), is well known for his confrontation with the prophets of Baal. Remember, these prophets were NOT from the nations around Israel. These were Israelites that had abandoned the worship of the one true God and had mixed the worship of God with paganism.

1 Kings 18:21

> [21] *Elijah went before the people and said, "How long will you waver between two opinions? If the LORD is God, follow him;*

but if Baal is God, follow him." But the people said nothing.

Just as it was at the time of Elijah, those most responsible for Israel going astray are its leaders.

Jeremiah 50:6

> [6] *My people have been lost sheep. Their shepherds [pastors?] have caused them to go astray. They have turned them loose in the mountains. As they have wandered from mountain to hill, they have forgotten where their home is.*

The northern kingdom has forgotten its roots, and it has not realized its purpose. It has left God's Torah (instructions) and has instead followed after other customs of other gods; all the while imagining that they are honoring God.

Ezekiel 36:25

> [25] *...I will cleanse you from all your contamination and your idols.*
> [26] *I will give you a new heart and put a new spirit within you ...*
> [27] *I will make it so that you will follow My decrees and guard My ordinances and fulfill them.*
> [28] *You will dwell in the land that I gave your forefathers; you will be a people to Me, and I will be a God to you.*

Although the northern kingdom may believe that THEY are the one's with the answers, God tells them that they should not just be humble, but embarrassed and ashamed.

> [31] *Then you will remember your evil ways and your deeds that were not good, and you will be disgusted with yourselves in your own sight because of your iniquities and because*

of your abominations.
[32] *Not for your sake do I act - the word of the Lord HASHEM/ELOHIM - let this be known to you! Be embarrassed and ashamed of your ways, O House of Israel.*

If there were an Elijah message for today, it would be no different then it has ever been; Repent (RETURN to God). Do not continue to mix the worship of foreign gods with the worship of the God of Abraham, Isaac and Jacob. CHOOSE who to serve, because the reunification of Israel is near.

But, HOW does the Bible tell us that they will return?

Jeremiah 3:14

> [14]*and I will take you one of a city, and two of a family, and I will bring you to Zion:*

They will NOT return because we discover their location or family genealogies. So why do they return?

Let's skim **Ezekiel 36** to see how this will happen:

> [17]*... The House of Israel dwelt in their own land, they defiled it by their own way and by their doings: ...*
>
> [19]*And I scattered them among the nations, and they were dispersed throughout the nations: ...*
>
> [21]*But I had concern for My holy name, which the House of Israel had profaned among the heathen, wherever they went.*
>
> [22]*... Thus says the Lord GOD; I do not do this for your sakes, O House of Israel, but for My holy name's sake ...*

[24]For I will take you from among the nations, and gather you from out of all countries, and will bring you into your land.

How is this accomplished?

[27]And I will put my spirit within you, and cause you to walk in my statutes, and you shall keep my judgments, and do them.
[28]And you shall dwell in the land that I gave to your fathers; and you shall be my people, and I will be your God.

Again, in **Jeremiah 31:33** it says:

This [shall be] the covenant that I will make with the house of Israel; After those days, says HaShem, ***I will put my law*** *in their inward parts, and write it* ***in their hearts****; and will be their God, and they shall be my people.*

If you are part of Israel this is the "sign" that God is calling you back; if you have a compulsion to observe his statutes and judgments.

Lets look again at **Exodus 31:13**

... You shall keep my Sabbaths: for it is ***a sign between me and you*** *throughout your generations;* ***that you may know*** *that I am HaShem that makes you holy (separates you).*

Notice, it is NOT a sign for others to see, but for ISRAEL to know that they are part of His holy people (the Hebrew word for holy is "kadosh" which means to set apart).

A spark within a person is somehow ignited, separating them from other people, as they are drawn to the study and observe of God's laws.

It may seem a bit confusing, because there is no way to

determine who will be drawn to do "Jewish" things and who will not, who will be compelled to keep the Sabbath and who will see no value in it, who will have a real love for the Biblical Holy Days and who will look at them as something strange.

However, the act of the House of Israel returning to God, is the event the whole world waits for. Even in the Christian Bible we see that Paul writes about this expected and anticipated event.

Romans 8:19

> *For the creation waits in earnest expectation*
> *for the manifestation of the sons of God.*

This phenomenon is also foretold the Jewish Torah Blessing.

Orthodox Torah Blessing

> Blessed are You, Hashem, our God,
> King of the universe,
> Who has sanctified us with His commandments
> and has commanded us to engross ourselves
> in the words of Torah.
> Please, Hashem, our God,
> sweeten the words of Your Torah in our mouth
> and in the mouth of Your people,
> the family of Israel.
> May we and our offspring
> and the offspring of Your people,
> the House of Israel - all of us -
> know Your Name and study Your Torah
> for its own sake.
> Blessed are You, Hashem,
> Who teaches Torah to His people Israel.

On Shabbat Teshuva (the Sabbath of Return) between Rosh

Hashanah and Yom Kippur the following line is added to the Amidah:

> *And in the book of life, blessing and peace, good prosperity, salvation and comfort, and good decrees, may be remembered and inscribed before You, we and all Your people, the House of Yisrael, for a good life and peace.*

In the blessing said EACH Sabbath before opening the doors of the ark (the place that the Torah Scroll is stored), are theses words:

> *And remember our brethren, the entire House of Yisrael in the lands of their dispersion, and walk them speedily upright to Tsiyyon Your city and Yerushalayim, the dwelling place of Your Name. As it is written in the Torah of Moses, Your servant: If you are dispersed at the outermost ends of heaven, from there, Adonai, your God, will gather you in and from there He will take you. Adonai your God, will bring you to the land that your fathers possessed and you will possess it. He will do good to you and make you more numerous than your forefathers.*

God is faithful at fulfilling His promises. At the end of the age the northern kingdom, (Israel), will return from exile, just as the Bible foretells. It is also something that the southern kingdom (Judah) has faithfully been expecting for thousands of years. Yet Israel's (the northern kingdom's) eyes have been blinded until this end time.

Fullness of Gentiles

Again, in the Christian Bible Paul writes in the book of "Romans" about "Jews" and "Gentiles" for the first several chapters. And then he begins to talk about Israel (the northern kingdom).

Romans 11:25

> *For I would not, brethren, that you should be ignorant of this mystery, lest you should be wise in your own conceits; that blindness in part has happened to Israel, until the fullness of the Gentiles has come in.*

What is Paul referring to when he says "the fullness of the Gentiles?" He is referring to an end-time prophecy that Jacob proclaimed on Ephraim, the younger son of Joseph in Genesis 48. Because Ephraim was the chief tribe of the northern kingdom, the House of Israel is often referred to as "Ephraim" in prophesy.

Genesis 48:19b

> *His younger brother shall be greater than he, and his seed shall become a multitude of nations.*

In this verse the words translated as "multitude of nations" are מלא הגוים (melo ha-goyim). The most commonly translated English word for "melo" is fullness. So, the words "multitude of nations" are more properly translated as "fullness of gentiles."

Paul is telling his Gentile readers that Israel is blinded and shall remain so until the time of this end-time prophecy made by Jacob. THEN their eyes will be opened and THEY SHALL RETURN! They shall be grafted back into the commonwealth of Israel to live a Torah lifestyle; and shall be reunited with their brothers from Judah.

This event will even over-shadow the exodus from Egypt.

Jeremiah 23:7

> [7]*Therefore, behold the days come, says the LORD, that they shall no more say, The LORD lives, which brought up the children of Israel out of the land of Egypt;*

> [8]*But, The LORD lives, which brought up and which led the seed of the house of Israel out of the north country, and from all countries where I had driven them; and they shall dwell in their own land.*

As we have seen, when the Bible says, "children of Israel" it is referring to all of Israel. However, when it refers to the "house of Israel" or the "house of Judah" it is referring to either the northern or southern kingdom. This prophecy in Jeremiah is about Israel, the northern kingdom, returning to God.

It is about the time we are NOW in. It is a time when Israel, who was lost, is now found. Don't misunderstand. Not all Christians are part of the Lost Tribes, nor are the Tribes all found in Christianity. The northern kingdom has been dispersed throughout the ENTIRE world and will return from every country and from every faith.

Finally, it is important to remember that a person is not more "spiritual" because he is required to observe more mitzvot (laws). Everyone is born to fulfill certain mitzvot. It does not make a lot of sense for a righteous Gentile to take on the entire "yoke" of the law. He is not required to do so. However, if he is part of the northern kingdom (the Lost Tribes) he will feel he has no choice but to do them.

So What Should We Do Now

If you are Jewish, help to make a way for the northern kingdom's return.

The House of Judah is the remnant that has been saved throughout history in order to guide the House of Israel back to the worship of the one true God at the end of the age. It is the House of Judah's OBLIGATION to guide the ten tribes (the House of Israel) back to God.

Zechariah 8:23

> [23]*This is what the LORD says, In those days, ten men, speaking all the languages of the nations, will take hold of the hem on the garment of a Jew and say, We will go with you, because we have heard that God is with you.*

Rabbi Yitzchak Ginsburgh, in his booklet The Seven Principles of Divine Service for Righteous Gentiles, writes:

> *Our generation is the first since the dispersion of the Jewish people in which the Jew is able (and therefore obligated) to reach out to the non-Jew.*

If you are a Gentile (Noahide) who has no desire to obey the laws any further than the seven noahide laws, you are fine. God will honor your reverence to Him and your loving kindness to others. Be a supporter of Israel and Judah and God will honor that support.

That was the original intent for those Gentiles who were joined to followers of "the Way" (later to become known as Christians).

Rabbi Jacob Emden (1697-1776) wrote about Christianity 300 years ago, and says:

> *You members of the Christian faith, how good and pleasant it might be if you will observe that which was commanded to you by your first teachers; how wonderful is your share if you will assist the Jews in the observance of their Torah. You will truly receive reward as if you had fulfilled it yourselves - for the one who helps others to observe is greater than the one who observes but does not help others to do so - even though you only observe the Seven Commandments.*

If, however, you are Israel, and you are part of this phenomenon discovering the faith of our Hebrew fathers, God is calling you back to himself. Like the prodigal son:

It is time to leave your pagan holidays and observances.

It is time to turn away from polytheism.

It is time to embrace God's Torah.

It is time to go to our brothers from Judah and say, "We have heard that God is with you."

It is time to come home.

Made in the USA
Coppell, TX
21 November 2019